ETHNICITY ON PARADE

✚ ✚ ✚ ✚ ✚ ✚ ✚ ✚ ✚ ✚ INVENTING THE
NORWEGIAN AMERICAN
THROUGH
CELEBRATION

April R. Schultz
✚

UNIVERSITY OF MASSACHUSETTS PRESS   AMHERST

LC 94-14810
ISBN 0-87023-939-2
Designed by Cora Lee Drew
Set in Palatino by Keystone Typesetting, Inc.
Printed and bound by Thomson-Shore, Inc.
Library of Congress Cataloging-in-Publication Data

Schultz, April R., 1962–
    Ethnicity on parade : inventing the Norwegian American through
celebration / April R. Schultz.
        p. cm.
    Includes bibliographical references (p.) and index.
    ISBN 0-87023-939-2 (alk. paper)
    1. Norwegian Americans—Ethnic identity.   2. Norwegian Americans—
Anniversaries, etc.   3. Norwegian Americans—Social life and
customs.   4. Ethnicity—United States—Case studies.
5. Americanization—Case studies.   I. Title.
E184.S2S38   1994
305.83′982′073—dc20   94-14810
                                                                    CIP
British Library Cataloguing in Publication data are available.

Contents

Illustrations

Acknowledgments

This book began as a term paper in a graduate seminar on popular culture in 1988. Since that early stage, many friends and colleagues have contributed generously of their time and resources, both intellectual and personal, to turning that paper into this book. While I take responsibility for any shortcomings in this work, any successes are certainly due to the advice, probing questions, and wisdom of many people.

This project would have been much more difficult to complete without the financial support of the University of Minnesota and Illinois Wesleyan University. The American Studies Program at the University of Minnesota awarded me a dissertation writing grant in 1990–91; in 1993, Illinois Wesleyan University supported a research trip to complete my revisions through a faculty development grant; and in the final, more mundane, stages of gaining photograph permissions and indexing, Dean Janet McNew of Illinois Wesleyan granted generous and much-needed support.

Early versions of this work were presented as papers at meetings of the American Studies Association and the Organization of American Historians. The final product benefited greatly from the comments of panel and audience members. Many of the archivists I met while writing both the dissertation and the book proved also to be invaluable resources. Along with thanking the people on the staff at the magnificent Minnesota Historical Society, I would like to thank more personally the archivists and officers of the Norwegian-American Historical Association and Archives in Northfield, Minnesota. Ruth Crane and Lloyd Hustvedt helped me enormously throughout this project. Though retired from her many years with the Historical Association, Charlotte Jacobson generously consented to translate an article for me. Odd S. Lovoll, editor of the NAHA's journal, *Norwegian-American Studies,* has also been very supportive of my work.

Various scholars, both friends and colleagues, read this book at different stages, and I owe them a great debt. I would first like to thank the 1989–90 American Studies Dissertation Writing Group—Joy Barbre, John Bloom, Amy Farrell, Michiko Hase, Jane Healey, Mark Hulsether, Scott Kassner, Chris Lewis, and Kate Spaeth. On Wednesday nights, they shared cookies, coffee, gossip, and, most important, their insights about my work and their own projects. Wendy Kozol, while finishing her own work long distance and beginning her teaching and research career, gave generously of her time reading and commenting on several chapters of this project. Betty Bergland not only shared her important work on ethnicity and immigrant women's autobiography, but also told me timely stories about her

Norwegian-American parents and grandparents. Each of these colleagues consistently pushed me to think beyond what I was already saying, and this book wouldn't be the same without them. My new colleagues at Illinois Wesleyan offered suggestions and encouragement in the book's final stages. I want to thank in particular Paul Bushnell, Brian A. Hatcher, Gordon J. Horwitz, Dianne Sirna Mancus, Pamela Moro, Patra Noonan, Georganne Rundblad, James Simeone, Michael W. Weis, and Michael Young.

I would also like to thank David Thelen, editor of *The Journal of American History,* and the anonymous readers who commented on and helped me to revise an article based on my early research. Their questions and comments at an early stage of this project helped me to conceptualize the historical importance of the celebration. For their comments and criticisms of more recent stages of this work, I owe a great debt to John Bodnar, David Glassberg, and Joseph T. Skerrett, Jr. My editor at the University of Massachusetts Press, Clark Dougan, has enthusiastically supported this project and offered welcome advice at every turn. Sharon Krauss proved to be a careful and sensitive copy editor, while Pam Wilkinson and Catlin Murphy helped me through the sometimes daunting production and promotion process. And thanks to Barbara E. Cohen for her careful indexing job.

My former teachers and colleagues deserve special thanks for different reasons. Michael Steiner, Karen Lystra, Leila Zenderland, and John Ibson first introduced me to American studies and interdisciplinary thinking at California State University, Fullerton. They have been continuously supportive of my work and have become valuable colleagues and friends. My professors at the University of Minnesota challenged me to think about American culture in new and exciting ways. Ellen Stekert helped me to confront folklore in my work and to think about cultural practice in that context. Rudy Vecoli pushed me to place this work in the large and changing context of immigration history. Riv-Ellen Prell helped me to think more deeply about the anthropology in my work and shared her own important work and insights about ethnicity. She has been an important teacher, friend, and colleague. Elaine Tyler May and Lary May pushed me to always think and write with historical rigor. David W. Noble made me forever sensitive to the way historians construct and shape history. He continues to be an important friend and confidante. Last, I cannot imagine this book without George Lipsitz, who has seen this project develop from a graduate seminar paper. His probing questions about the meaning, context, and politics of popular historical narratives pushed me to think about ethnicity in compelling ways. His example as a teacher and a colleague who deeply believes in the political importance of scholarship was instrumental in my beginning my academic career and completing this work.

I owe my family a special debt. My parents, Rose and Les Gottlieb and Gary and Diane Schwenneker, gave me encouragement, timely visits, and a sense of perspective. From my first day in graduate school, I have shared this adventure with Bob Schultz, my partner and colleague. We've shared frustrations, successes, dirty dishes, even a computer. He has not only nurtured me with his presence (and his cooking), but has also pushed me to be precise and ground my work in the "concreteness" of history.

Lastly, I want to thank my grandmother, Velma Hamilton, who taught me the importance of stories. She told her grandchildren many stories about our collective past—about her grandfather who rode with Sherman's army; about her great-uncle who defied his family and married a Cherokee "princess"; about her mother-in-law who drove a covered wagon alone from Iowa to Kansas; about her missionary aunts who saved a group of children during the Boxer Rebellion in China; and about our ancestor, Jane Hartin, who fled the Irish potato famine alone as a young girl. Whether these stories were "true" or not, I've come to understand their significance as a gift from a grandmother to her grandchildren; these narratives constructed a past that transcended her own constricted life as the wife of a poor farmer in a patriarchal culture. They told of adventure, independent spirit, and the importance of difference. Her stories and her avid interest in politics, history, and literature instilled in her children and grandchildren an independence that she realized only when she stole the time to read. I dedicate this book to her.

✛ ✛ ✛ ✛ ✛ ✛ *ETHNICITY ON PARADE*

Prologue

The *"Pageant of the Northmen"*

✦ ✦ ✦ ✦ ✦ ✦

O n a cold, windy Minnesota evening in June 1925, approximately fif-teen thousand spectators gathered at the state fairgrounds in St. Paul. This audience watched from the grandstand bleachers as fifteen hundred Norwegian Americans performed in a grand spectacle that was part his-tory lesson and part fairy tale.[1] The *Pageant of the Northmen* was a stirring, melodramatic account of Hans Christian Heg, a Norwegian immigrant and Civil War martyr. Lavish scenes of immigrant settlement, suspenseful contact with Native Americans, triumph over innumerable crises—partic-ularly the Civil War—and community celebrations and growth would have been recognized by an audience familiar with early twentieth-century civic pageantry in America.[2] As in Anglo-American progressive pageants, the history of brave, industrious, and virtuous pioneers would reawaken simi-lar values in the audience, who would carry them off into a revitalized future.

The *Pageant of the Northmen*, however, began not with pioneer settle-ment, but sometime in the 1830s with a little boy in Norway listening at his mother's knee to heroic and romantic tales of the Norwegian past.[3] The grandstand grounds were transformed into a stage area marked on three sides by a screen of shrubbery. The entertainment started with a scene of the Heg family inn situated to the left of the stage area and surrounded by the cast of fifteen hundred figures spanning a thousand years of Nor-wegian history and folklore. As these Vikings, trolls, folk dancers, politi-cians, ministers, soldiers, inventors, and pioneers marched to the pageant overture and disappeared behind the shrubbery, ten-year-old Hans Heg carried firewood up to his family home. His mother, sitting at her spinning wheel on the stone walk, grabbed Hans to her and stroked his hair. Ac-cording to the pageant manuscript, she "looked into his blue eyes [and]

Fig. 1: A woman and child ready for the Centennial celebration in traditional "peasant" costume. *Courtesy Norwegian-American Historical Association.*

thought she saw pictures of new lands. Her mother's heart would hardly let him go. . . . She must hold him while she could."[4]

Sensing his mother's prophetic mood, Hans asked her for some folk tales, and the audience was treated to familiar legends as trolls, gnomes, witches, and fairies danced to Mrs. Heg's pantomimes. Dancers in brightly embroidered vests and colorful hats—traditional "peasant" dress—performed as the storyteller reminisced about such youthful dances after working in the fields. Such stories evoked a period in Norwegian history, from roughly the 1840s to the 1870s, when the simmering romantic nationalism of the turn of the century boiled over into a full-fledged movement. Artists, poets, scholars, and nationalists retrieved and cultivated a heritage of common "folk" whose stories of otherworldly spirits and peasant victories over aristocracy provided a link to the pre-Danish Viking past and stirred a Norwegian identity separate among the Scandinavian countries. In 1814, Norway achieved independence from Denmark, but immediately yoked itself to Sweden, which essentially ruled until Norwegian independence in 1905. Romantic nationalism was a defining movement throughout the nineteenth century and enjoyed a resurgence after 1905 not only in Norway, but also among immigrants in the United States.[5] The pageant dramatics, therefore, would have been very familiar to the audience.

It was left to Hans's grandfather to develop for the spectators the connection between these nineteenth-century folk traditions and the Viking past. He entertained the boy—and the audience—with heroic legends of Vikings in battle; of Leif Ericson "discovering" the New World and soundly defeating a group of unfriendly Indians; of Olaf Tryggvesson raising a cross and Christianizing the violent and pagan Viking warriors. The Viking Olaf was Christianized in England after a raid on the British Isles and returned to Norway to bring Christianity and to gain political control. He died in battle in 1000 and the job of Christianizing was continued by his kinsman, Olaf Haraldson. This St. Olaf reigned for fifteen years, establishing Christian laws and practices. Opponents allied with the Danish successfully to dethrone St. Olaf, who was killed in battle. As Norwegians came to regret Danish rule, St. Olaf became a symbol of Norwegian nationalism and independence. The connection between nationalism and Christianity in the figure of St. Olaf was both supported and reinforced by the religious revival of the early nineteenth century led by Hans Nielsen Hauge, a pietist lay preacher whose experiential Christianity was followed by an increasingly active rural peasant class. The spectacle on stage reminded the audience of these important links between nationalism, Christianity, and pagan traditions.

It was to the "reality" of the nineteenth century that the pageant then turned as Hans's father recounted more recent events. He reminded his son—and the audience—of young Cleng Peerson, who in 1821 sought his fortune in America, bought land from Indians, and staked out claims in the

Fig. 2: Pageant publicity photograph juxtaposing a Viking explorer, likely Olaf Tryg-gvesson, and two monks, signifying the Christianization of the pagan Vikings. *Courtesy Minnesota Historical Society.*

Midwest, and of a group of fifty-one Haugean and Quaker Norwegians who in 1825 followed Cleng Peerson on a "sloop" called *Restaurationen* and successfully settled in the new land. While a few Norwegians had immigrated to the United States before, this celebrated beginning in 1825, made even more mythical by the birth of a girl en route, marked the official beginning of Norwegian immigration. This original fifty-one would become eight hundred thousand by 1925. As Mr. Heg finished his tales of Peerson and the "sloopers," Ole and Ansten Nattestad, just returned from America, stopped by the Heg family inn to describe the great opportunities awaiting them in America. The Hegs agreed to join the next group to sail, continuing the long tradition of Norwegian adventurers before them.

Norwegian emigration followed a pattern similar to other European countries in the nineteenth century, in which structural changes encouraged movement from farm to city, and from country to country. The percentage of the Norwegian population to emigrate was second only to Ireland's. There were three waves of Norwegian immigration to America—the 1860s, the 1880s, and the 1900s. During each of the periods, conditions including slowing industrial development, increasing population, low trans-Atlantic fares, connections in America, and the condition of the American economy, combined to draw immigrants interested in either advancing or maintaining their material status. The "sloopers," who emigrated primarily for religious reasons, were unique among Norwegians who followed.[6] The pageant ignored the more mundane aspects of this history, focusing instead on an almost mystical adventurousness of early pioneers in search of freedom and opportunity.

The audience watched as the Norwegian scene was transformed into an unidentified "American forest" at some earlier time. Spectators were then treated to an ill-fated love story about young Indian sweethearts from hostile tribes. The girl's tribe captured her love and prepared to burn him at the stake, despite her pleas to the chief. As the executioners "perform[ed] a wild dance," a white missionary arrived, stamped out the fire, reunited the couple, and sent them away. When he set up a cross and knelt to pray, the Indians followed his lead, listening intently as he spoke of "the great spirit" and "the cruelty" of Indian ways.[7] The pageant audience was reassured, then, that a painless Christianization had already occurred by the time the first settlers reached the forest. When the immigrants appeared, weary from their long journey, they paced off boundaries and proceeded to share a meal. After prayers, the sleeping pioneers dreamed of

Fig. 3: Pageant participants pose for a publicity photograph. *Courtesy Minnesota Historical Society.*

nymphs—"spirits of the wood"—and woke the next morning to encounter the Indians, who, according to the pageant directions, "have heard that they are to leave these woods and they are to hold a final impressive ceremony." As the Indians worshiped, the Norwegians "look[ed] on in wonderment" and then approached with their guns. The chief, however, gave a sign of peace and communicated their imminent departure. The settlers, in turn, "describ[ed] how they [would] plow the ground, cut down the trees, and build houses."[8] Finding this plan reasonable, the Indians offered the Norwegians a peace pipe, again reassuring the audience with a smooth, seemingly inevitable transition from "savagery" to civilization.

Though some Norwegians settled in Chicago and Minneapolis, the majority continued their rural life, helping to settle the Midwest, first in Illinois and Wisconsin in the 1830s, and later Minnesota, Iowa, and the Dakotas. Norwegian settlers were drawn to the wooded areas rather than the drier plains, but paid the price of settling in the damp woods with cholera and malaria epidemics. They also continued to live in the vicinity of Indians, and, though relations between the groups were often peaceful, violence punctuated the period of settlement.

Following the Indians' fictional departure, the Norwegians welcomed new immigrants, including the Heg family, and they proceeded to build their community in a pattern that was familiar to each new group of Norwegian settlers. The audience watched their ancestors' counterparts chop logs, saw wood, and shoe horses. They heard cowbells as the settlers built a church in the ever more idyllic community. They saw the first child born and baptized, cholera kill a mother and child, the first confirmation class, and beautiful young women courted by handsome young men. As in the Anglo-American pageants, such scenes established the settlers as sturdy, temperate, pious people who were able to overcome extreme hardship to reproduce those values in the next generation.

And, like other pageants, this production depicted the Civil War as a pivotal moment in the community's history. These scenes began in the 1850s when Hans Heg was a Free Soil candidate for the state legislature. Hans was engaged in a debate with his Irish-American opponent when a group of fugitive slaves arrived, bound for Canada. He invited the slaves to the platform and asked them to sing some "plantation songs," which they did. A group of southerners arrived and showed Heg their papers. Not wanting to break the law, the Norse settlers unwillingly turned over the slaves, who sang "Nobody Knows the Trouble I've Seen" as they were led off the stage. Heg then "stir[red] his audience to a patriotic fervor" as he spoke out against slavery.[9] This scene not only established Heg as a

Fig. 4: Abraham Lincoln and other cast members posed around Colonel Heg's casket for a publicity photograph. *Courtesy Minnesota Historical Society.*

hero, but reminded the audience that Norwegians were truly democratic and egalitarian, more so, surely, than Heg's Irish-American opponent.

The threat of war was broken by Hans's wedding to a young woman named Grunhild. Guests performed traditional dances and the famous Norwegian violinist, Ole Bull, played a traditional bridal song. Such a scene assured the audience that the community will survive despite impending disaster. The Civil War intruded, however, when a stage driver arrived, shouting in Norwegian and English, "Fort Sumpter is bombarded!" Simultaneously, on another part of the stage, dancers performed a "military ballet" to give "expression to the sentimental and poetic aspect of the imminent conflict." A young man passed in front of the store, shouting in Norwegian and English, "President Lincoln calls for volunteers!" As the scene ended, some of the men formed a squad and marched out. Hans Heg took charge of the famous 15th Wisconsin, made up of Norwegian immigrants. General Grant arrived to award Heg his colonel's commission and the two conferred over maps. The pageant then reenacted Colonel Heg's death in the Battle of Chickamauga; the poignant death scene closed on General Grant and President Lincoln standing behind Heg's bier.[10]

The last scenes of the pageant, culminating in the grand finale, reminded the audience of the great successes of Norwegian Americans in the New World, successes built upon the shoulders of heroic pioneers and patriots like Hans Heg. After Heg's tearful funeral, a minister, a choir, and a confir-

Just a Few of the Things To Be Seen and Heard
FROM O. M. NORLIE
COLLECTION   at the

NORSE-AMERICAN CENTENNIAL

Celebration and Exposition

Minnesota State Fair Grounds
June 6-7-8-9, 1925

Four Big Days---Continuous Program
Educational---Entertaining---Inspiring

HEAR

Hon. Calvin Coolidge, President of the United States.

Hon. Frank B. Kellogg, Secretary of State of the United States.

Hon. H. H. Bryhn, Norway's Minister to the United States.

Rt. Rev. J. P. Lunde, Bishop of Oslo, Norway.

And other official representatives of Norway, Iceland and the Dominion of Canada, also U. S. Senators, Congressmen and Governors of Norse ancestry.

Hear the following famous musical organizations:

Academic Choir (50 voices) from Norway
St. Olaf College Choir and Band
Luther College Concert Band
Augsburg Seminary Glee Club
Concordia College Choir
Augustana College Choir
Waldorf College Choir
Norwegian Singers' Association Male Chorus
Prominent vocal and instrumental soloists.

SEE

The immense, colorful Historic Pageant with 1,000 people taking part.

The beautiful "Living Flags" of Norway and the United States, by 420 school children.

The full size model of the sloop, "Restaurationen," (the Norwegian "Mayflower").

The Prize-winning models of the ancient Viking ships.

The wonderful Norse woven Tapestries, worth thousands of dollars.

The baseball and tennis games, soccer game, and big program of athletic contests and races.

The official exhibits of the natural resources of the State of Minnesota and Dominion of Canada.

The many paintings and sculpture by famous Norwegian and Norse-American artists.

A veritable "world's fair" of interesting exhibits in 22 different departments, including wonderful collections of old Norse relics and those from pioneer days in America —actually thousands of articles of historic value and interest.

An Opportunity That Comes But Once In A Lifetime! You Can't Afford To Miss It!! Buy Your Tickets Now!!!

Fig. 5: A publicity flier announcing the upcoming Centennial. *Courtesy Norwegian-American Historical Society.*

mation class marched in, faced the audience, and retreated to the back of the stage. As they left, a college president and his male and female students marched in, saluted the audience, and joined the first group. They were followed by groups representing art and literature; invention, industry, and commerce; World War I soldiers, Red Cross nurses, and women war workers. All held their positions for the last scene, which was the occasion for unveiling a statue of Hans Heg, "who proved himself all that is highest in the citizen of a republic and who gave his life in battle for his adopted country." The pageant manuscript stated that ancient kings and Vikings appeared, "as in a dream . . . sturdy immigrants, slaves, soldiers, and spirits, all gathered, reminding the audience of all the strange characters who had had an influence upon the colonel's life."[11]

This elaborate spectacle of Norwegian-American history and identity was the culminating event of a four-day celebration that drew over two hundred thousand participants to the Twin Cities from throughout the United States and Canada. Commemorating the arrival of the *Restaura-*

tionen in 1825, the Norse-American Immigration Centennial was an event that rivaled the most successful state fair in attendance to date. Prior ticket sales numbered 124,140, so large a number that in early spring the Centennial committee had to squelch rumors that there were no rooms left for visitors in the Twin Cities. Events included religious services in both Norwegian and English, sessions in both languages devoted to introducing dignitaries from Norway and the United States—including President Coolidge—music performances, and exhibits of Norwegian and Norwegian-American history, art, cooking, crafts, heirlooms, and industrial inventions. Organizers interspersed orations, religious services, parades, exhibits, music, and pageantry into a massive historical display. Like the pageant that ended it, the Centennial was a merging of history and mythology. Far from a simple celebration, however, the Centennial was part of a significant effort to reinvent a Norwegian-American ethnicity suitable to the context of 1920s America. What ended in the pageant performance was a negotiation among various forces in the community that offered to the participants a complicated and contradictory vision of the past and, therefore, of their present and their future.

1

Ethnic Identity and Celebration: An Introduction

✦ ✦ ✦ ✦ ✦ ✦

In the Centennial's souvenir program, Professor O. M. Norlie asserted, "It might be said that every nation is a peculiar people, called of God to perform a peculiar service for mankind. The Norwegian people in times past have been called to perform a great mission in the world. . . . they have been the bearers of personal independence and liberty under law, they have been champions of the home and the school, the church and the state." Norlie concluded, "The Centennial will renew and enforce the faith in our precious heritage."[1] As this statement demonstrates, the "peculiarity" of Norwegian Americans as outlined by Norlie was clearly compatible with middle-class American ideals. Indeed, Centennial organizers argued that Norwegian Americans, descendants of Viking explorers who not only had discovered America but had conquered much of northern Europe, were *better* Americans than "Yankees" were. From the perspective of the Centennial's middle-class organizers, the celebration was a process of cultural legitimation. Their representation of Norwegian-American ethnicity was "safe" and nonthreatening to American business, politics, and culture in the 1920s. Such a "safe" vision would allow these organizers to maintain their positions as ethnic leaders in an ethnic community without challenging American ideology. In many ways this celebration of progress paralleled dominant Anglo-American progressive history in its emphasis on expansion, individuality, and linearity. This representation, however, was based on a use of the past that rendered the organizers' conservative narrative highly unstable and contradictory. The Centennial celebrated not American progress, but Norwegian-American progress. A historical memory of Norwegian romantic nationalism subverted the organizers' narrative and inverted the dominant assimilationist ideology. The Centennial was not merely a commemoration of an immigrant ship, but a complex process of invention, of creating Norwegian-American ethnicity.

The celebration took place in the immediate context of "Americanization"—an intense effort by political, civic, and cultural leaders to deal with what Theodore Roosevelt called "those evil enemies of America, the hyphenated Americans."[2] The drive to Americanize the immigrants did not simply lead to a clash between Americanizers and the ethnic community, but brought to bold relief a debate among the Norwegians themselves over the very identity of that community. Most historians of the Norwegian-American experience argue that the crisis engendered by Americanization in its most virulent form during World War I ended in the 1920s with an ethnic "counter-reaction" that was merely a "final mustering" of nostalgic forces before an inevitable merging with American society. For many of these historians, the Centennial, with its invocations to patriotic Americanism, was the "counter-reaction's" paradigmatic event. World War I Americanization had "worked"—it merely accelerated an inevitable progression from Norwegian to American.[3]

The evidence, however, points to a more complex and contradictory conclusion. Out of the great tensions, conflicts, and negotiations over what it meant to be a Norwegian American amidst the politics of Americanization and nativism, Centennial organizers and participants arbitrated a complex cultural identity. The complexity of this process reveals not only that Norwegian Americans were anything but monolithic, but that historical discussions of Americanization require a fuller analysis of these often overlooked debates and that historical evidence seeming to embrace Americanization involves many, often contradictory, interpretations. A particularly significant time to explore, 1925 signified not the end of a viable Norwegian-American community, but a time when Norwegian Americans *appeared* to be Americanizing rapidly while still choosing to celebrate their ethnicity in a very public way. Historians and social scientists often seek to contain and "control" such contradictions by explaining them away, by focusing on the "closure" of events in order to arrive at a smooth narrative of history and human behavior. Thus, historians of the Norwegian-American experience explain the conservative nature of the Centennial as a nostalgic ethnic counter-reaction that, through its Americanization rhetoric, epitomized full assimilation. What such an interpretation misses is the "inventedness" of ethnicity and the questions that such a concept would pose.[4]

From such a vantage point, ethnicity is not inherent but is constructed as

Fig. 6: Descendants of the "sloopers" posed before a model of the 1825 immigrant ship, *Restaurationen. Courtesy Norwegian-American Historical Society.*

a dialogue between immigrants and dominant society. It is not something to be preserved or lost but rather is a process of identification at a particular moment to cope with historical realities. Hence, the decline of an "ethnic" community reveals not that immigrants have assimilated as much as it reveals that these people have found other strategies to cope with changing historical conditions. In what contexts, then, is ethnicity invented? What power relations are embedded in, created out of, and / or challenged in that process? How does a community construct an identity out of competing definitions and concrete concerns? How do class, gender, folklore, memory, and history merge and become embedded in such an event as the Centennial in the name of "ethnicity"? And, most difficult to answer, why, among the many other options for constructing identities, do people at certain historical moments choose ethnicity as a signifier of identity?

The larger lesson to be gained from the Centennial and the surrounding debates in the Norwegian-American community is that assimilation and Americanization were hotly contested. They were not—and are not—

monologues of the groups in power, but multilayered and ongoing dialogues that are part of the larger creation and re-creation of cultural identities. In her analysis of revisionist studies of the "public sphere," Nancy Fraser proposes a notion of "subaltern counterpublics," or "parallel discursive arenas where members of subordinated social groups invent and circulate counterdiscourses to formulate oppositional interpretations of their identities, interests, and needs."[5] The Norwegian-American Centennial offers a strategic site for studying such creativity, for the contradictions and tensions revealed in this cultural activity prove that ethnicity is not static, but changes over time as a result of efforts to negotiate those contradictions and tensions.

Thus, a study of the ways in which the 1925 Centennial shaped ethnic identity among Norwegian Americans might lead to some important generalizable principles about ethnicity, especially in respect to commonly voiced assumptions about the ease and inevitability of assimilation. An examination of how ethnicity is expressed in a popular cultural event among middle-class white ethnics—rather than in ethnic institutions, in literature, or among racial minorities whose challenges to assimilation are highly visible—reveals how historical narrative, historical memory, literature, folklore, festivity, class, and gender all contribute to the construction of complex and contradictory cultural identities.[6] The complicated tensions emanating from the construction of ethnic identity out of complex relationships and historical memories often elude even the best scholars of ethnic experience. By acknowledging and analyzing these tensions, we see that such an effort prefigures an alternative cultural world and discloses the instability of the dominant assimilationist narrative itself. Therefore, if assimilation was such a contested process among Norwegian Americans—a white, predominantly middle-class, Protestant ethnic group—then we must strongly question the still standard assumptions about the "naturalness," and thus, inevitability, of ethnicity and assimilation in both scholarly works and in our popular imagination.

In *Immigrant Women in the Land of Dollars,* Elizabeth Ewen argues that, until recently, immigration historians have tended mainly to "chart the journey from miserable beginnings to great success," the end product of which was, either implicitly or explicitly, complete assimilation into American life.[7] Influenced by the work of sociologists, earlier Robert Park and later Milton Gordon, and beginning with Oscar Handlin's seminal work, *The Uprooted,* these historians sought to find the key to unity out of diversity. How did immigrants overcome the pain of being uprooted and torn from the culture of the Old World to become Americans? The assumption, of course, was that this was a natural and inevitable process. Later supported by the work of mobility historians, the commonplace thought was that as immigrants and their children moved up and out of the working class, they would meld into American culture, with only vague though cherished memories of an ethnic past.[8] The story told by historians of the Norwegian-American experience reflects this larger narrative of immigration history and has been little influenced by more recent works in the field.

A newer generation of social historians has focused on the resourcefulness of ethnic groups. The best of these works avoid the static and sharp dichotomies—between a static Old World culture and an equally static American culture—of the older scholarship. John Bodnar's major synthesis of immigration history is perhaps the best example of this new work. Bodnar argues that immigrants confronted the American capitalist system pragmatically, utilizing their traditions to "creatively construct their own cultural world," a world that helped them to confront their present situations.[9] In a recent collection of essays edited by Virginia Yans-McLaughlin, historians, sociologists, and political scientists offer a "new paradigm" for immigration history that rests on two related premises. First, it places immigration to the United States in the context of a global labor market and expanding world capitalist economy. Second, it focuses on collective rather than individual strategies for meeting this social situation. The "new paradigm" therefore challenges both a linear assimilationist model and American exceptionalism.[10] Such work demonstrates that the immigrant world was not a replication of the culture they left behind, but a complex creation that had a great deal to do with the circumstances of migration and settlement.[11]

As Olivier Zunz has put it, from these findings "we are beginning to understand assimilation as a complex interactive process in which immigrants are not merely unwitting beneficiaries of a growing set of opportunities." But Zunz and John Higham (in a slightly different way) have reacted largely to works that argue for the important similarities that unite diverse ethnic experiences. Zunz claims that the new advances "make it difficult to return to the assimilationist view inherent in the majority of mobility studies, but there are also limitations inherent in the view stressed more recently of a pluralistic America fragmented into an endless number of autonomous communities." Zunz's answer is to look at "those large-scale factors that cut across ethnic, economic, or political loyalty to influence people's lives."[12] Higham, on the other hand, offers "pluralistic integration," a "nexus . . . between individual rights and group solidarity, between universalistic principles and particularistic needs." Although, as Higham points out, pluralistic integration depends on "a general acceptance of complexity and ambiguity," at bottom it is an effort "to revitalize a common faith amid multiplying claims for status and power."[13] While Higham and Zunz's works are important and often convincing endeavors to deal with the real problems of particularistic studies, their scholarly endeavor is still to find the key to American unity.

The works of social historians who study immigrant ethnic communities offer significant and persuasive correctives to such efforts to return to a unified and homogenous view of American culture. They are, nonetheless, in many ways embedded within an assimilation narrative. The assumption still operative is that as the community takes on bourgeois patterns of material wealth and leisure, ethnicity wanes dramatically. Though Bodnar's immigrants utilize their traditions to "create" a new culture, that culture is implicitly transitory, for they "ultimately would acquiesce in the new order of urban capitalism. . . ."[14] Even in a new collection on immigration history that calls into question both American exceptionalism and the linear assimilation model, the underlying assumption of many of the contributors is that they are describing a process of "adjustment," which connotes a transformation to something "normal" and static.[15] Furthermore, the very definition of what it means to be ethnic remains relatively unchanged in these works. For the "ethnic" portion of these immigrants' lives is based on a seemingly "primordial" and therefore natural set of values and beliefs. When these "primordial" values are no longer in evidence, ethnicity is no longer operative. Too often, immigration historians assume what they should be proving. They accept assimilation and its closures as the truth without seeing the rhetoric and practices of assimilation as a historical strategy masking quite unstable and inconclusive ethnic identities.

Historians of the Norwegian-American experience are prone to generalizations embedded in such assumptions about the nature of ethnicity and assimilation. Minnesota historian Carl Chrislock, for example, contrasts the 1925 Centennial with the 1914 Eidsvoll Celebration in the Twin Cities, which commemorated the one hundredth anniversary of Norwegian independence from Denmark. The activities of the two celebrations were similar but, for Chrislock, the 1914 festival symbolized ethnic revivalism and an openness to difference in the larger culture, at least for white ethnics. The Eidsvoll festival not only focused on a Norwegian national celebration but emphasized "ethnic maintenance" among the immigrants, and the Norwegian language predominated. The "mood generated by the observance" intensified the drive to expand Norwegian language instruction, and ethnic fraternal societies increased their recruitment campaigns.[16] At the time of the Eidsvoll festival, asserts Chrislock, "very few observers were predicting that assimilation would shortly obliterate the Norwegian-American community," when World War I helped to slow ethnic activism and "festival rhetoric became considerably more prone to acknowledge the claims of American patriotism." Indeed, for Chrislock, the 1925 Centennial was merely "a last hurrah"—the end of Norwegian-American history.[17]

Chrislock's evidence for this death knell is the predominance of the English language and assimilationist rhetoric—or exhortations to patriotic Americanism—at the Centennial. Likewise, Odd Lovoll refers to the Centennial as "the last rally—an ethnic counter-reaction." In his view, the event provided a "grand rallying point" for those Norwegian-American organizations struggling to gain their lost momentum. However, in his view the Centennial didn't succeed in reestablishing with full force the preservationist concerns of these groups. Rather, "the festival was a nostalgic retrospective view. Many spoke warmly of what Norwegian-Americans had achieved, but the prospects for a flourishing Norwegian-American culture were dim. The 1920s, therefore, represent a final mustering of strong Norwegian ethnic forces."[18] But because those forces did not lead to an increase or revitalization of ethnic *institutions*, the Centennial was, to Lovoll, essentially assimilationist.

Chrislock's and Lovoll's interpretations are not idiosyncratic. From the earliest historical works to recent monographs, historians of the Norwegian-American experience have placed this period within a larger narrative of assimilation.[19] In general, these historians view the Norwegian-American community during the period from the late nineteenth century up to 1924 as a specifically "Norwegian-American" culture, that is, as a transitional "bridge" between the Norwegian being left behind and the American to come. In his sweeping history of the Norwegian people in America, Theodore Blegen in 1940 argued that the immigrant struggle was the struggle to achieve a "unified cultural personality," a struggle within which Norwegian-American culture "played a mediating role." The Norwegian American, living in both the Old World and the New, was, according to Blegen, "on the bridge of transition. . . . He adjusted himself to American ways, not by some instantaneous or magical transformation, but idea by idea."[20] Forty-four years later, in another sweeping history of Norwegians in America, Odd Lovoll argued, "Norwegian Americans—in the manner of other ethnic groups in America—were pulled between two cultures, the one they had left behind and the one they had to gain a foothold in. They thereby tried to embrace both while moving inexorably toward integration with American society."[21] With striking consistency, historians of the Norwegian-American experience chronicle a process of assimilation, moving from ethnic strength and solidarity up to 1914 when World War I created a crisis in the immigrant community, and ending most often in the 1920s with a nostalgic ethnic "counterreaction."

While anthropologists and cultural critics require the empirical rigor and contextual depth offered by historical accounts, social historians need anthropology and cultural studies to see how vibrant and contradictory seemingly static evidence can be. Building on Fredrick Barth's notion about the primary significance of the creation and maintenance of ethnic boundaries as well as the permeability of those boundaries, anthropologists have challenged earlier assumptions about both the self-contained nature of ethnic groups and the inevitability of assimilation.[22] According to these scholars, what is important is not the relative levels of "traditional" cultural values and behaviors, but how a group ascribes to those values at different times and for different reasons. Patricia Albers and William R. James, for example, argue that "what is generalizable about ethnicity . . . is not the saliency of specific ethnic label(s) and varying relationships. Rather, it is the stereotypic process by which people differentiate and label themselves in relation to others. It is also concrete circumstances and dynamics of social relationships between groups that inform the underlying process of ethnic differentiation."[23] In many ways, this is reminiscent of historian Orlando Patterson's argument about the "use value" of ethnicity—that ethnicity is "used" by groups in competition with each other for scarce resources.[24] But there are larger issues at stake than a conscious manipulation of ethnic referents for political gain. E. L. Cerroni-Long, for example, argues that the use of ethnicity is always ideological and not always conscious. Not only is it part of ethnic boundary formation and maintenance, but it should be analyzed as part of larger ideological movements in the context of "the social, economic, political and administrative reality of the national setting in which [it] emerges."[25] Ethnicity, then, is a dynamic process of self-definition that must be studied in the specific historical context in which that self-definition takes place.

Literary critic Werner Sollors has made a provocative attempt to analyze ethnicity in American culture as invented. In his introduction to a volume of essays titled *The Invention of Ethnicity,* Sollors proposes that "the interpretation of previously 'essentialist' categories (childhood, generations, romantic love, mental health, gender, region, history, biography, and so on) as 'invented' has resulted in the recognition of the general cultural constructedness of the modern world." In terms of ethnicity, the use of "invention" would be to "suggest widely shared, though intensely debated, collective fictions that are continually reinvented."[26] While Sollors's interpretation of ethnicity is a significant corrective on essentialist examinations of "authentic" cultures, his view suffers from what anthropologist Renato Rosaldo has called the "postmodern problem of weightlessness."[27] Sollors abstracts ethnicity from historical circumstances, posing an egalitarian, pluralistic vision of democracy in which everyone has equal access to any narrative. He makes no attempt to analyze how, under what historical circumstances, and why ethnicity is invented in the first place.

Both the anthropologists' notions of the "use" of ethnicity and Sollors's concept of invention imply self-conscious, pragmatic—and therefore painless—manipulation. But the "use" of ethnicity arises out of struggle, loss, and concrete historical experience. As anthropologist Michael Fischer compellingly argues, "Ethnicity is not something that is simply passed on from generation to generation, taught and learned; it is something dynamic. . . . it can be potent even when not consciously taught . . . something that emerges in full—often liberating—flower only through struggle." Out of this struggle, continues Fischer, comes the "discovery of a vision, both ethical and future-oriented." These visions "can be both culturally specific (e.g., the biblical strains of black victories over oppression) and dialectically formed as critiques of hegemonic ideologies (e.g., as alternatives to the melting pot rhetoric of assimilation). . . ."[28] In this way, both the cultural content of ethnicity and its use are not only grounded and significant but change over time, allowing instead of assimilation a dynamic model of both accommodation and resistance.

The Norse-American Centennial Celebration offers a rich "case study" for the kind of creativity Fischer suggests. The Centennial was not part of an inevitable and therefore natural progression from a static Norwegian culture to a full embrace of Americanism, but part of a complex dialogue at a historical moment of struggle within the Norwegian-American community. Furthermore, that struggle was not merely an effort to assimilate, nor to preserve intact a Norwegian world view. Rather, it was in many ways an effort to redefine the parameters of ethnic identification. Out of the tensions between Norwegian and American cultural structures, the Centennial posed an inversion of the dominant story about the inevitability of progress and the necessity for complete Americanization, an inversion that fully challenged the prevailing assimilationist ideology. In Fischer's terms, the Centennial was the occasion for the community to invent an identity that was both "culturally specific" in its exhortations to a heroic Norwegian past and "dialectically formed" as a critique of the hegemonic assimilationist ideology. Accordingly, ethnicity may be seen as a continuous hegemonic struggle between a dominant society and the social experience of marginal and subordinate groups.[29] The Centennial, then, may be interpreted as an act of resistance *and* negotiation.[30]

Furthermore, such a symbolic construction of ethnicity was not a homogenous identity invented and accepted by a homogenous group. What the Centennial demonstrates is that ethnicity is part of ongoing "identity-making," both individual and communal. The Norwegian Americans who organized and participated in the Centennial were members of a "community" only at varying levels. Some lived in and were involved in ethnic neighborhoods and ethnic institutions. Others lived in regions where there were very few Norwegian Americans, yet they identified strongly with their peers of Norwegian origin and ancestry. In addition, the community was often divided along lines of class, gender, and definitions of Norwegian-American ethnicity. Meaningful talk about identity, both communal and individual, requires thinking of identity in terms of efforts to "control, stabilize, or explore meanings," as "ongoing identity-work" that is historically situated.[31]

Anthropologists have understood longer than historians that celebrations and public events are significant sites where meaning is reaffirmed and/or constructed.[32] In this view, festivals and celebrations are a function of the dynamic relationship between the group that is celebrating and the group in power. Depending on that relationship, the celebration will be oppositional or supportive of existing institutions.[33] Susan G. Davis, in her study of nineteenth-century street parades and ceremonies, thinks "historically about culture and anthropologically about history" to demonstrate that "public enactments" are not just reflections of society, but are rhetorical "political actions" that "are not only patterned by social forces, [but are] part of the very building and challenging of social relations."[34] In his recent study of twentieth-century commemorative events, John Bodnar argues that "public memory is produced from a political discussion that involves not so much specific economic or moral problems but rather fundamental issues about the entire existence of a society: its organization, structure of power, and the very meaning of its past and present."[35] Because ethnic identity in a multicultural society is inextricably linked to the ethnic group's relationship to the larger society, ethnic celebrations are important sites for examining the construction of ethnicity. Until recently, historians of the ethnic experience have paid little attention to the role of celebration in ethnic communities, except as nostalgic "local color" or, in the immigrant generation, as a vehicle for ethnic maintenance. A historian's perspective, however, is crucial if we are to avoid the often static notion of a "model" that is so prevalent in anthropology. The Norwegian-American celebration, for example, was both supportive of existing institutions *and* oppositional. However, while we can locate the "model" in which this celebration fits, this does not tell us how or why the community constructed such a celebration. By first understanding the significance of celebration and then placing that celebration in its historical context, we can analyze the ways in which ethnic identity is invented as well as the meaning of that invention.

The Centennial did not transform participants from one identity to another; nor did it signify the "death knell" of Norwegian-American ethnicity. The "language" of the Centennial was part of an ongoing and complex statement about and construction of Norwegian-American identity. By focusing too often on an assumed linear progression from ethnic to American, immigration historians have missed these significant moments of creativity. This study will therefore question many of the standard assumptions about the inevitability and linearity of assimilation. But it will also contribute to a growing body of scholarship about the invention of culture, about the efforts of people to reinvent their pasts in ways that can both legitimate and challenge the realities of the present. Ethnicity, then, must be understood not as nostalgia for a perceived authentic past, nor as a symbolic invention divorced from historical realities. It must be understood instead as a historically grounded act of cultural politics.

— 2 —

"To Lose the Unspeakable":
Negotiating
Norwegian–American Identity

✦ ✦ ✦ ✦ ✦ ✦

For historians of the Norwegian-American experience, World War I and its attendant Americanization "worked"; that is, it merely accelerated an inevitable progression from Norwegian to American. Though this scholarship amasses a rich narrative of Norwegian-American culture in the twentieth century, the "facts" of the narrative are constructed according to specific assumptions about ethnicity, assimilation, and social change that limit the narrative's complexity.[1] Convinced of the desirability of assimilation, these historians read back into the past an inevitability that distorts the real historical choices, desires, and struggles of Norwegian Americans at the time. They view ethnicity as a static and finite construct, and they determine the "stage" of assimilation according to the "authenticity" of the group's ethnic forms. If so-called Old World values are no longer visibly utilized to survive in the American environment and if ethnic institutions are on the decline, then the group is reaching a state of assimilation with an equally static American culture. The periodization of Norwegian-American history is grounded in this assumption, which is itself predicated on particular ideas about social change. On this broader level of social change, the historians of Norwegian-American history chronicle a closed hegemonic process. Though the Norwegian-Americans in these narratives have a thriving ethnic culture for a time, it is merely a transitional culture—a bridge to becoming fully American. Then, when the dominant culture decides that even "safe" northern European immigrants must Americanize, the Norwegians hasten the process and assimilate. Even some of their own join the ranks of the Americanizers. In this scenario, the dominant culture's hegemony is complete.

The evidence, however, reveals conflicts and tensions that these historians have ignored. If we shift our view of culture and social change to a process of contestation and negotiation over meaning between dominant and subordinate groups, hegemony appears much more elusive and incomplete. Rather than hastening a foregone conclusion, the crisis engendered by World War I can be viewed as part of a continuing, long-standing debate and negotiation over ethnic identity, both between the dominant culture and the Norwegian-Americans and among members of the ethnic group itself.

In his 1955 study, *Strangers in the Land: Patterns of American Nativism,* still considered the most comprehensive work on the subject, John Higham amassed a great deal of evidence into a powerful narrative chronicling Americanization and nativism. His evidence demonstrates that while nativism during and after World War I was its most nationalistic and strident, it had had a long history in the United States, beginning at least with the Alien and Sedition Acts in the 1790s. According to Higham, nativism in its many forms developed in earnest after the Civil War and waxed and waned thereafter, ending, one supposes, in the late 1920s when Higham ends his own narrative. Higham locates moments of most profound nativism in times of social dislocation brought about by economic depressions, while moments of egalitarian pluralism occur in times of economic growth and opportunity. While Higham's portrayal of deep fear and threat at times of economic and social upheaval makes some historical sense, this relatively contained definition of nativism denies larger patterns of prejudice that have important implications. Higham's interpretation does not acknowledge that nativism and the assimilation ideology are part of a much larger western narrative that began at least with the age of exploration. As one French scholar has eloquently claimed, since the conquest of the American continents, "Western Europe has tried to assimilate the Other."[2] The power of this narrative has been immense, and American nativism should be viewed as one manifestation of this story.

The hegemonic Americanization narrative naturalized the conflict between the American self and the "other," and historians of this process largely perpetuate that narrative. But the "other" is always there, pushing at the boundaries and threatening the hegemony. As Jewish intellectual and ethnic preservationist Horace Kallen put it, the Americanizers' "demand is not for the conservation of personality, for freedom of variation, for the ordering of institutions so as to insure to men's souls their autonomy and integrity. [The Americanizer] requires that individuality shall be submerged in conformity, that conformity shall be blind, and shall fall continuously in with the unseen and imprevisible changes of the ancestral conventions and mores of the American village community as these are appreciated and understood by the masters of this community." Fortunately, Kallen pointed out, this push to conformity "has never existed unopposed."[3]

Americanization ideology was a hotly contested terrain. Many Norwegian Americans, for example, fought to keep the word "Norwegian" in the Norwegian Lutheran Church of America rather than conform to a unifying synod; they founded societies like *For Faedrearven* (For the Ancestral Heritage) in direct response to Governor Harding's call for "English Only" in public places; and they fostered the immigrant press and immigrant literature—all in the context of World War I, the Red Scare, and the longer restrictionist movement. The strength and often violence of the Americanization movement speaks to both the threat posed by ethnic groups and the nativistic need to destroy that threat in order to resolve and preserve an American identity.

The history of Americanization and nativism is a long and complicated one. In the years between the Civil War and World War I, the tolerance of immigrants vacillated between bland acceptance and direct hatred. At times, even Anglo-Saxon racial nativism masked itself as an egalitarian ideology. Many Americans in the post–Civil War era, invoking cosmopolitan and democratic ideals, believed deeply in the benevolent process of assimilation. America could accomplish two goals at once, according to this ideological sleight of hand. First, the country could maintain its image as an asylum for the oppressed. And second, these "oppressed" could successfully merge and mix with native-born Americans to produce an even more superior race according to Spencerian evolution. Of course, there was also an economic pay off—the ever-expanding industries would be guaranteed a continuous and cheap labor supply. As Higham puts it, "Anglo-Saxon and cosmopolitan nationalisms merged in a happy belief that the Anglo-Saxon has a marvelous capacity for assimilating kindred races, absorbing their valuable qualities, yet remaining basically unchanged." The key word here, of course, is "kindred." It was easy to maintain a belief in the beneficent powers of the melting pot as long as the bulk of immigrants hailed from northern Europe. When Anglo-Saxonists lost "faith in the process of assimilation," immigrants became viewed as "a distinctly national menace."[4]

The loss of faith in the assimilative powers of American culture became evident in the late 1870s and early 1880s. Labor struggles, agricultural crises, and the formation of radical organizations paralleled the growth of the factory system and city slums, leading some reformists to take a new and serious look at immigration. Class conflict, both in the factories and in agriculture, bred fear of foreign radicals and the emergence of a more visceral racial nativism. This was compounded by the beginnings of a massive "new immigration" from southern and eastern Europe. In an 1881 letter to the *New York Tribune,* the writer argued that "the nation has reached a point in its growth where its policy should be to preserve its heritage for coming generations, not to donate it all to the strangers we can induce to come among us."[5] The immigrants were no longer easily assimilable "kindred races." In his sociological study of 1914, E. A. Ross argued that with the new immigration, "it is reasonable to expect an early falling off in the frequency of good looks in the American people. It is unthinkable that so many persons with crooked faces, coarse mouths, bad noses, heavy jaws, and low foreheads can mingle their heredity with ours without making personal beauty more rare among us than it actually is." He applied the same reasoning to issues of "stature and physique," "vitality," "morality," and "natural ability."[6]

This brand of nationalism from the 1870s to World War I varied in intensity depending on the perceived economic health of the country. Depressions, of course, made labor strikes and general anxiety more likely, whereas periods of general prosperity saw a relative absence of nativistic diatribe. But it was always present, lurking either as a general and vague fear or in specific legislative proposals to restrict immigration. In either case, nativism grew steadily and became more and more complex in its critique of immigration. Reformers linked problems of urban life to the concentration of immigrants in ghetto communities. Though some recognized that the slums were more a sign of devastating structural circumstances, others focused on the assimilability of the immigrants themselves. In other words, if they were truly assimilating, they wouldn't live in these conditions. Other middle-class reformers in such movements as temperance and women's suffrage often referred to the immigrants' "backward" ideas about these issues. Economists argued that immigrants lowered the workers' standard of living and that immigration restriction would alleviate labor strife and chaos. This myriad of complaints about immigrants refueled such organizations as the Immigration Restriction League, which lobbied for several different restriction acts from 1875 to 1924 with varying success, depending on the larger nativistic climate.[7]

Such attitudes focused almost exclusively on southern and eastern Europeans, Irish Catholics, Asians, and blacks before 1914. Questions of ethnic maintenance versus assimilation, however, were also being discussed within northern European, Protestant ethnic groups, the Norwegians not the least among them. As John Bodnar points out, these debates were not unusual. "Essentially," he argues, "the balance of power in the United States . . . was shifting and fragmented before World War I. The nation-state, a growing business class, regional and local interests, and the concerns of ordinary workers, immigrants, and farmers all asserted themselves vigorously."[8] The Scandinavians occupied a generally favorable position on the "kindred races" scale. In Minnesota and much of the upper Midwest, pre–1914 attitudes "gave wide latitude to ethnic diversity." Indeed, Minnesotan political and business leaders, recognizing early on the need for population to stimulate the economy, had worked hard to attract immigrants, particularly Scandinavians and Germans. Ethnic differences and tensions surfaced over issues such as prohibition, public schools, and religion, but "politicians found it inexpedient to crusade against groups armed with voting power, and the private sector maintained a healthy respect for immigrant market power."[9] As with German Americans, the general acceptability of Norwegian immigrants as potential Americans ironically encouraged an assertion of a specifically ethnic culture that challenged American culture and served as a direct threat during World War I.[10] Such seemingly benign issues as language-use flew directly in the face of Americanization ideology, making Norwegian Americans vulnerable to intensified nativism. In this period, ethnic organizations ranging from mutual aid associations to regional societies to language-preservation leagues began and flourished. Debates over language-use in churches, schools, and secular societies began in earnest, though the Norwegian language continued in strength. Ethnic-centered politics grew in this period, and by 1917 the Norwegian Americans were arguably the most powerful ethnic minority in the upper Midwest in terms of regional and national political participation. And a small body of Norwegian-American literature addressed larger issues of ethnicity and Americanization exemplified in these more specific aspects of immigrant life.

Before 1900 and the growing urbanization of Norwegian immigrants, the Lutheran church was the most important ethnic institution—and the most contentious institution—in the immigrant community. Unlike the Swedes, for example, who had only one Lutheran synod, the Norwegians in America founded fourteen Lutheran synods between 1846 and 1900. The formation of these various synods were based on theological differences, which were not unusual in American immigrant churches, but which had in common a powerful meaning and presence for Norwegians in America.[11] As with other immigrant churches, the Lutheran churches were the bases for social activity and communal aid in Norwegian settlements. The proliferation of different synods provided a home for immigrants that linked them to their homeland religion. As one scholar puts it, the church "was the only institution (except the family) which the immigrants could reestablish relatively unchanged in the new environment, and so served as the chief bond with their premigrative past."[12] Synod affiliation, in addition, seemed "to be influenced by [the] regional, cultural and social class backgrounds [of clergy and laity] in Norway."[13] Such circumstances reinforced both the power of the Norwegian clergy and the segregation of Norwegians from other Lutheran immigrants.

In the period from 1900 to 1914, the membership in Norwegian-American secular societies grew approximately four times, from fifteen thousand to sixty thousand, paralleling the growing urbanization of the Norwegian communities.[14] The growth of these ethnic organizations and secular societies could be attributed in part to the fact that a third great wave of emigration from Norway occurred between 1900 and 1910. This was largely an urban immigration and the Sons of Norway and social groups based on county and district origins (the *bygdelag*) would likely have attracted many new immigrants. But the tremendous growth should also be viewed in the context of larger cultural patterns. Many northern European ethnic groups flourished in this period in terms of ethnic-centered activity. Their relative immunity from the nativism that did exist in this period may explain this heightened activity. But they were not completely immune, either from Americanizers in the larger culture or from those within. The agitation over language-use, for example, was indicative of pressures from both within and without. The organization and successful existence of these groups must also be viewed as part of the larger struggle over ethnic identity.

The three most successful organizations in terms of longevity and membership were the Sons and Daughters of Norway, the *bygdelag*, and *Nordsmanns Forbundet*—the Norsemen's Federation. The Sons of Norway was founded in 1895 by eighteen working-class Norwegians in north Minneapolis and soon grew to national proportions. Basically an urban organization that would become by far the largest secular society of Norwegian Americans, the Sons of Norway had mutual aid as its original goal. Members paid for unemployment benefits and funeral expenses, and the organization later expanded to provide other types of insurance. In 1897 a Daughters of Norway was founded and in cities where there was not a female counterpart, women were allowed to join the Sons of Norway. The two merged in 1950 under the latter name. The lodge was for the most part made up of laborers and lower-middle-class Norwegians. Among the leaders in its early years were many who were also active in political reform movements, including socialist organizations. The Sons of Norway became a power center second only to the Norwegian Lutheran Church.[15]

Organized at almost the same time as the Sons of Norway, the *bygdelag* began as a regional picnic at Minnehaha Park in Minneapolis. All from a particular district in Norway, these individuals came together to celebrate a reunion. This original meeting sparked the *bygdelag* movement: by 1910 twelve *bygdelag* had been organized and by World War I there were fifty groups nationally. The organizations focused on Norwegian regional identities. Each *lag* held annual reunions where the members celebrated regional dialects, food, folk tales and arts, music, and humor. Some published yearbooks and many joined other *lags* to organize larger festivals such as the 1914 Eidsvoll festival and the 1925 Immigration Centennial. While the *bygdelag* had rural "peasant" origins, they attracted members from all over the political, religious, and economic spectrum. The only qualification was the desire to reunite with people from one's home village or district.[16] By the 1920s, many in the *lag* movement saw themselves taking over the task of ethnic solidarity from the church, which was embroiled in efforts to meet the demand for English in its services. One *lag* member, for example, argued, " 'It is so deadly quiet within the Norwegian church. Quiet as a deathbed. And the day is not far away when the church will conduct a merry funeral for Norwegianess.' "[17]

Whereas the *bygdelag* were based in regional identities and the Sons of Norway focused on concrete financial needs of immigrants, *Nordmanns Forbundet*, founded in 1907, focused on fostering unity between Norwegians in America and in Norway. An outgrowth of Norwegian independence from Sweden in 1905, the organization's main goal was "to maintain the connection and strengthen the unity between Norwegians in and outside of Norway and to gather men and women of Norwegian ancestry in all parts of the world for joint work for Norwegian culture and Norwegian interests."[18] By 1914 the organization had approximately twenty thousand members in North America and nearly the same number in Norway. Its members played host to Norwegians visiting America and particularly to Norwegian Americans visiting Norway. To publicize this "joint work," *Nordmanns Forbundet* published ten periodicals a year on both Norwegian and Norwegian-American topics.

Many smaller associations that focused on Norwegian and Norwegian-American history, current issues, and literature proliferated in this period, paralleling these larger organizations. For example, The Norwegian Society in America was founded in 1903 to unite "all Norwegian Americans around the worthwhile causes of Norwegian language, literature, and immigrant history."[19] Partly because of its inability to shed its elitist image, the Society had only four hundred members by 1914. The Society dedicated itself to maintaining the Norwegian language and awarded stipends to Norwegian-American artists and writers. Its main achievement, however, was the publication of *Kvartalskrift* (Quarterly) from 1905–1922.

This journal became in part a forum for a dialogue over issues of pluralism and assimilation, a dialogue that permeated both Norwegian-American literature and institutions. This was evident in the beginning when the very purpose of the Society was debated by Johs. Wist and Waldemar Ager, the journal's editor. Wist argued that the purpose of the Society was to act as a link to Norwegian culture, easing any intellectual deprivation in the inevitable shift from one culture to another. The Norwegians in America would need to foster their heritage until their "descendants in the second, third, or fourth generation have become assimilated, and, as an integral part of the nation, can more exclusively nurture themselves on its cultural fruits."[20] In his response, Ager disagreed that the Society's main purpose was to nurture a Norwegian heritage. Rather, its purpose was to help *create* a new culture from *Norwegian-American* experience by preserving what was precious and valued from Norwegian culture. "If we admit that we now are in transition from one nation to another, then our saga will only be written in a way to indicate that we have left independent cultural traces which mirror our own lives, our own struggles. We know full well that ethnic groups in this country have become completely assimilated without leaving their cultural traces, but we also acknowledge that this is sad indeed and of little honor to their nationality."[21] Ager's goal was to forestall this event by fostering a strong and vital Norwegian language and literature through the Norwegian Society in America.[22]

Language was the fulcrum around which much of the debate in the community took place. For example, in 1905 Ager sermonized on language use in *Kvartalskrift* in an article entitled "Preserving Our Mother Tongue." He wrote, "A goodly number seem to think that the Norwegian language is only suited for the 'old man' or the 'old woman,' that the ones who want to advance in this country had better slip into the new conditions and become Americanized as quickly as possible. To do this they must shake off everything that reminds them of a foreign culture as soon as practicable." Ager goes on to argue that the greatest number of successful Norwegian Americans in politics and literature were born in Norway, not in America. The second generation hadn't distinguished itself because, in Ager's view, they had been denied the "character" that comes from knowing "a mother tongue tied to pride in family and race."[23] Perhaps no one voiced this position more powerfully than author O. E. Rolvaag. In a speech given on the Fourth of July 1903 (later published in a series of fictionalized letters to Norway), Rolvaag lamented that the losses suffered by emigration had been much greater than the gains. The greatest loss was the

> intimate spiritual association with our own people and our own nation. . . . [We are not just] strangers among strangers, *but we came away from our own nation and became strangers to our own people.* . . . We have thus to be a harmonizing part of a great whole; we have become something by ourselves, something torn off, without any organic connection here or there. . . . In short we have become rootless. . . . We lost that which does not permit itself to be expressed in words, *we lost the unspeakable.* The saddest of all is that we do not comprehend these things until it is too late. Could, in truth, the people in the old country see it as you and I see it, it would not be long until the stream of emigration would be nearly dried up (Rolvaag's italics).[24]

The immigrant's pain is most profound in this passage. For Rolvaag, to "lose the unspeakable" was to lose one's culture, the "life-vision"[25] that gave meaning and depth to everyday existence. Intellectuals like Ager and Rolvaag argued that endemic in language was an immutable national personality without which the Norwegian American was lost. Some claimed otherwise. Editor Luth. Jaeger, for example, argued that young people cannot "divide themselves and be both Norwegian and American without harming their development as American men and women." They don't need to deny their ancestors and heritage, but they also don't need to accept a "mess of Norwegian pottage." Writer P. P. Iverslie, who had grown up in America, disagreed. His own experience as a bilingual in both language and culture gave him a "wider horizon" in which to behave and judge events.[26]

This intellectual conversation over *Sprogsporsmaalet*, or the Language Question, grew out of concrete, often bitter, controversy within families, neighborhoods, and institutions such as the schools and the church. In his massive study of the Norwegian language in America, Einar Haugen found that "the heart of the matter was the family; this was the primary battleground" over language-use. The family, supported by the church and the neighborhood, strongly resisted "any attempt to lessen their sociocultural role."[27] Although Norwegian language-use lasted much longer in cohesive rural communities than in urban environments, the battle deepened as children in each area came more and more into contact with English. The poignant struggle between children and their immigrant parents is well documented in studies of various ethnic communities and in ethnic literature. In *Peder Victorious*, Rolvaag's second novel in the *Giants in the Earth* trilogy, the author eloquently recounted this struggle between child and parent that was embedded in language. In a letter to Percy Boynton about the novel, Rolvaag wrote, "You will agree with me, I think, that it is a tragedy for mother and child not to be able to converse intimately with each other. Her songs he cannot understand. What her soul has found nourishment in, he cannot comprehend. . . . There are tragedies in life for which language has no expression—this is one of them."[28] Though written in the 1920s, the novel takes place in the late nineteenth century in rural North Dakota. Beret's son Peder begins school and comes into contact not only with a teacher bent on Americanization but with the children of Irish-Catholic settlers. As the distance between Beret and her son grows, she realizes that "America would not be satisfied with getting their bodies only! . . . Hidden forces were taking the children away from her."[29] For Beret, language was the very expression of her subjectivity—it was what defined her as a human being and its loss in her children separated her from them in a profound way. This novel rendered a very real struggle, which only strengthened in the late nineteenth century as the public school system spread and communities became more diverse.

This intimate pain found a larger voice in institutional deliberations over the use of language. The Lutheran church provided the primary justification for Norwegian language-use outside the family. It was not only a site of struggle over theological issues, but, as in the family, over language as well. For most of the nineteenth century, the Norwegian churches in America provided the majority of instruction for reading and writing in Norwegian. Church leaders wanted to unite immigrants and to establish parochial schools dedicated to the preservation of Norwegian language and, therefore, Norwegian culture. The Norwegian Synod, founded in 1853 and considered most closely connected to the State Church of Norway, took the lead in theological disputes, and in the debates over language-use and parochial schools. As public schools made inroads in the Midwest, disputes over language began in earnest. The church was touched by this in several ways. For example, their parochial schools were threatened by the 1889 Bennett Law in Wisconsin requiring that a certain amount of English be spoken in all schools. At the same time, some young church leaders, witnessing the flight of young people from the church, began to argue that a transition to English was inevitable and the church should play a role in making that transition as smooth as possible. Others still argued for complete preservation. But by 1915, one-quarter of all the sermons in the Norwegian Lutheran Church were conducted in English, certainly an advance from no sermons delivered in English in 1900. The church eventually became bilingual and then increasingly English but not without prolonged and bitter discussion.[30]

As the literature and the documented debates suggest, many people tied language inextricably to cultural identity, viewing the increasing use of English as signifying a complete loss of any Norwegian-American culture. The convergence of language-use and the parochial school issue was a powerful example of this fear. Norwegian clergy, viewed as the central community leaders both in Norway and in the American environment, engaged in long battles over the "American School" from 1870 to 1920. For many clergy and their laity, the "American School," as it was referred to in clergy discussions and in literature, was a direct threat to their traditions, to the sense of order they had established in the New World. They believed that cultural maintenance—one of their primary goals—was not possible without knowledge of the Norwegian language and high culture. Other clergy defended the "American School," arguing for an assimilation in which "Norwegian" values of democracy, independence, thrift, and so-briety would mingle with "American" values and help to elevate and change "those elements of American life which are crudest and most wretched . . . drinking and carousing . . . [and] that peculiar American 'cleverness' which should be regarded with scorn and disgust by every noble Norwegian."[31] Such statements by a self-proclaimed assimilation-ist like Professor Georg Sverdrup of Augsburg Seminary were common among those clergy and laity more interested in temperance societies than in parochial schools. But such activity, in many ways linked to larger pro-gressive politics, also belied a particularly "ethnic" identity, as Sverdrup's statement suggests.

In the context of language disputes and efforts at cultural preserva-tion, such statements suggest strongly that the Norwegian-American com-munity was steeped in tension and debate over their place in Ameri-can culture. For example, rather than being a transparent sign of ethnic power and maintenance, the urban secular societies established after 1900 were often begun in response to diminishing language-use and should be viewed as part of the continuing negotiation over Norwegian-American identity. Many organizations such as the Norwegian Society in America had language preservation as their primary concern. But even societies like the Sons of Norway, foremost a financial institution, had as one of its secondary goals the preservation of the Norwegian language. The "secular counterpart to the church," these institutions were part of an ongoing, often bitter, dialogue.[32] This dialogue was often specifically over language-use, but as the evidence suggests, language-use was a signifier for larger issues of cultural identity.

This sense of struggle and change is particularly evident in the Norwegian-American literature of this period. As Dorothy Skardahl argues in the only large-scale study of Scandinavian-American literature, most authors fell in between the extremes of a total rejection of either Norwegian or American culture. No one who lived through the process of immigration "underestimated its difficulties. . . . [Novelists] showed all first- and many second-generation characters aware that their dual heritage made them indelibly different from native-born Americans in some respects."[33] How the differences were portrayed depended on the author's attitude about assimilation and ethnic maintenance. Two early examples of such literature in the Norwegian language are the novels of Drud Krog Janson and her husband, Kristofer Janson, who was already a well-known author by the time the two immigrated to Minneapolis in 1882. Both were actively involved in reform movements, including women's suffrage, in Norway and America.[34]

Drud's late nineteenth-century novel, *The Saloonkeeper's Daughter,* was a romantic novel of manners based largely on her experience as an immigrant. In *The Saloonkeeper's Daughter,* Drud addressed her own feelings of estrangement in the narrative of Astrid Holm. Astrid immigrates to Minneapolis with her father, who opens a saloon. She is unhappy but cannot escape, for her father is interested only in business and finds no time to deal with his daughter's troubles. She is constantly fighting off the drunken Norwegians in the saloon, and the Norwegians outside the saloon are not much better. They, like her father, are narrow-minded and interested only in accumulating capital. Astrid is influenced deeply by the lecture of a visiting Norwegian intellectual and nationalist, Bjornsterne Bjornson (a good friend of the Jansons'). Upon his urging, she becomes a Unitarian minister committed to women's rights. For Astrid, salvation comes from the Norwegian world of ideas rather than from the petty materialism of the immigrants she sees around her; they have become the epitome of American greed and individualism.

In *Behind the Curtain,* also published in the late nineteenth century, Kristofer Janson critiques American culture on many different levels: its refusal to accept the immigrants on their own terms; the ill treatment of women; capitalist insensitivity and greed; and the poor conditions of laborers. The novel's nouveau-riche Americans, the Plummer family, lack Culture. But worse, they are insensitive buffoons who would rape women, bribe juries, and cheat workers without a thought. Juxtaposed to the Plummers are many different Norwegian-American characters. The Plummers' first maid, Agnes Pryst, is a well-educated, talented musician from a cultured Norwegian family; the second maid, Dina Nilson, is a virtuous young woman who is raped by her employer's son, Frank; Dina's father is an outspoken anti-capitalist laborer who connects his daughter's rape and Frank's crooked acquittal with speculative, predatory capitalism. When Dina commits suicide, her father hangs himself. The Plummers find him hanging by a porch rafter, a note pinned to his shirt: "You have killed my life's happiness; you have killed my child; you have killed me. You have taken away everything I own—now take my corpse with it. I present it to you at bargain rates. The rope which you have bound around my neck will one day twist around yours and that of all millionaire robbers, who live on the tears of widows and the drudgery of workingmen." The double funeral occasions a workers' demonstration against the capitalist elites and soon after, Frank commits suicide. In response to his son's death, Mr. Plummer claims that Frank just had too much heart, which is "no good— no good—for business."[35]

Both of these highly melodramatic novels should be read, of course, in the context of progressive social protest literature.[36] But issues of ethnicity are ever present in these novels, which are thus part of the larger discourse on Americanization and ethnic preservation in these years before World War I. In *The Saloonkeeper's Daughter,* the Norwegians in America have given themselves over to materialism and greed, a theme that is reminiscent of other Norwegian-American social-realist fiction. In this novel, the saloon was clearly established as an "American" institution which symbolized materialism, godlessness, urbanization, and industrialization—all evils against which justice-, freedom-, and equality-loving Norwegian-Americans must fight. The only answer for Astrid in this environment is to cultivate a Norwegian culture, both intellectual and nationalistic. In *Behind the Curtain,* both educated and working-class Norwegians are virtuous human beings who meet with rebuke and violence in their encounters with American culture. In a visit to Norway in 1906, Rolvaag gave a speech on "American Social Conditions" that paralleled the ideas in both Jansons' work. "I have thought much on why it is that the life of the Norwegian American is so poor in true and genuine inner happiness. . . . Neither the Yankee nor the Norwegian American has been able to determine the proper relation between earning money and using it in the interest of human well-being."[37]

While authors such as Ager, Rolvaag, and the Jansons viewed such conditions as evidence for the need to maintain and cultivate a Norwegian heritage, others argued for assimilation, albeit in a peculiarly "Norwegian" fashion. In his 1914 novel, *Harold Hegg*, Reverend M. F. Gjertsen linked this "fight" against American degradation to Americanization. In a speech at the state capital, Hegg outlines his " 'progressive ideology.' " Gjertsen alerts his audience that Hegg, like many Anglo-Saxon progressives, opposes immigration from southern and eastern Europe because of the lengthy time it would take for this "lowest element" to become Americanized. On the contrary, according to Hegg, Norwegians have quickly become good American citizens because they brought with them from Norway "our race's impulses for freedom, independence, trustworthiness, and deep respect for law and order." Thus, Hegg argues that only full assimilation will allow these values to permeate and benefit American society, chiding those who insist on maintaining the Norwegian language, for "their feeble mind is weakened steadily by their dreaming, sickly yearning for Norway. There is neither success nor progress in such a sentiment. . . ."[38] Whether arguing for maintenance or assimilation, however, the positive "Norwegianess" that is presented not only by the Jansons and Rolvaag but by Gjertsen, is based on a sense of cooperation and a cultivation of values that stand starkly against American predatory capitalism. Whether this is "true" is a moot point here. What is important is the very utterance of such beliefs. Not all Norwegians in America were worried about the degradations of American capitalism or even about the loss of the Norwegian language. But the fact that those addressing a Norwegian-American audience in novels, essays, and speeches counted on the acceptance of such ideas by some of their public indicates that there was in process an important dialogue about what it meant to be Norwegian in America.

3

"The Day of the Great Beast": World War I, Americanization, and a Community in Crisis

✠ ✠ ✠ ✠ ✠ ✠

In a moving passage from his 1920 novel *Pure Gold*, O. E. Rolvaag poignantly addressed the transformative effects of World War I on Norwegian-American ethnicity, Americanization, and nativism.

> Everything about her spoke of American efficiency. Take her name, for example—Hazel Knapp, so short and with such a snap to it, with no trace of foreign origin, neither in sound nor in spelling. . . . There was hardly a soul in America to whom the World War gave greater moments of exaltation; it inspired her so. Her enraptured enthusiasm changed into religious worship to which she surrendered herself completely. How could she help it? The war was so mighty, so beautiful, so noble. Hazel saw clearly that an era of sweet brotherhood was dawning upon a sick world. . . . America had been chosen by God to lead the war, her country and its noble Allies! . . . To her there were only two classes of people: the real Americans who in her terminology included those who saw the war through her eyes, and on the other hand these—these-well— these infamous foreigners who invariably had pro-German leanings.[1]

In the context of World War I, the Red Scare, and a widespread campaign for "100% Americanism," Rolvaag's novel serves as evidence of the tensions within his community over cultural identity. In an article two years earlier, the author had declared, "Everything that is not of Anglo-American origin has been rendered suspect to an ominous degree. . . . In some places ill will and suspicion turned into the most rancorous persecution. . . . All that was strange was dangerous; so it had to be extirpated. They were not particular about the means, and woe to anyone who tried to object."[2] Though Americanization movements had a much longer history, World War I exacerbated and accelerated American nativism into an often hysterical and paranoid nationalism. In many ways, *Pure Gold* is the narration of this experience.

Later in the chapter, Rolvaag has Hazel meet with defeat in her efforts to raise money for the war when she approaches the Houghlums, who refuse to give even the smallest amount. When Hazel relates her defeat to some boys in town, they offer to help.

> "What do you want done to Mrs. Houghlum?" one asks.
>
> "Oh, how can I tell?" she cried in dismay. "If I were a man and not just a helpless woman, I wouldn't be asking you. . . . I'd teach her and that old skinflint of a husband of hers a lesson in patriotism that they'd never forget—they are a disgrace to the whole state!"
>
> "Do you mean for me to go and hang them, Hazel?"
>
> "I don't care, Roy. Just so you teach them what it means to be an American these days!"[3]

Roy's reference to hanging speaks to the tremendous violence associated with the drive to Americanize the immigrants and the parallel move to purge America of radicalism in 1919–1920.

Yet Rolvaag does not construct his novel as a simple story of virtuous Norwegians attacked by American patriots. His satirical description of Hazel Knapp and his reference to lynching take place within a chapter apocalyptically titled "The Day of the Great Beast." The "beast" does not merely refer to World War I and its attendant nativism, but evokes the "beast" within. For Hazel is herself Norwegian, as is Roy. The Houghlums' refusal to give money to Hazel does not stem from the anti-war sentiment shared by many Norwegian Americans, but rather from a lust for money that leaves them completely bereft of any sense of community. A twofold irony underlies the exchange between Hazel and Roy. "What it means to be an American these days" boils down to complete conformity and vigilante violence. Hazel has learned this lesson well. But the Houghlums need no lesson. In Rolvaag's view they already know "what it means to be an American." Indeed they are a parody of "American" materialism and greed. Rolvaag presents all of the characters in the novel as lacking any deep sense of ethnic identity; his project is not so much to repel attacks from outside as it is to reveal corruption from within. He hoped that this novel would demonstrate what happens "to an individual who has no tradition and no cultural background" and to argue on behalf of ethnic preservation and cultivation.[4] Thus, *Pure Gold* reveals the tensions over being Norwegian American in the context of Americanization and nativism.

This postwar novel echoes Rolvaag's early assessment of the Norwegian community in America. From his emigration as a young man in 1896 to 1901, he kept a diary in which he first addressed these issues. In an entry dated June 13, 1900, Rolvaag wrote of his early encounters with his fellow Norwegians in America: "Again, I have tramped about another day and have met with none but crippled souls. They are dead, dead, living dead! Their highest interests are hogs, cattle, and horses. . . . The spiritual life, received of God as the most precious gift, is dead. The sense of beauty, with which they might perceive the wonders and glories of nature, and the beauty in life, has been killed by the cold hand of materialism."[5] The most potent imagery in this passage is the "living dead," which in Norwegian folklore is the worst kind of troll, a being condemned to haunt the earth for his sins during life. For the young Rolvaag, these sins included turning away from the "spiritual" values of Norwegian life to a life devoted to material gain. Rolvaag believed that the Norwegian Americans lacked a true spiritual and cultural community because they had turned away from their heritage. If that culture could be revitalized and strengthened, however, the Norwegians could improve their own lives as well as contribute to an American culture that, in Rolvaag's eyes, was greatly lacking itself. These issues had always concerned the author and teacher, but the war and its attendant nativism spurred him to action, beginning with *Pure Gold*. Without a vital "Norwegianess" to sustain them, the characters in *Pure Gold* are destined to either Hazel's blind, vacuous patriotism or the Houghlums' empty greed. These traits, Rolvaag implies, made them particularly vulnerable to the propaganda and persecution of World War nativism. For Rolvaag, the only answer—for both Norwegians and Americans—was to revitalize Norwegian-American culture.

Pure Gold illuminates not only Rolvaag's position in the debate over Americanization, but also the complexity of the debate itself. It is crucial that Hazel Knapp and the Houghlums' are Norwegian Americans who have clearly forsaken their own culture and succumbed to both greed and Americanizing propaganda. One colleague of mine, a third-generation Norwegian American, tells the story of her father, who went to school during this period. His teacher would not allow the children to speak Norwegian, even on the playground. In defiance, they would retreat to the cornfields to carry on conversations in their native language. What makes this story all the more significant is the fact that the teacher compelled to Americanize her pupils was the little boy's Norwegian-American sister. The family spoke Norwegian in the home, but the pressure to Americanize in the public schools was very strong. The young Norwegian-American teacher may have been required to enforce an English-only rule, or, like other individuals in her ethnic group, she may have been sympathetic to the efforts of educational reformers to create a national norm. In either case, the incident highlights the complexity of the Americanization debate.[6]

Such stories clearly demonstrate that the drive to Americanize the immigrants did not simply lead to a clash between the Americanizers and the ethnic community, but brought to bold relief a debate among the Norwegians themselves over the very identity of that community. Indeed, in his 1916 *Atlantic Monthly* article, "Trans-National America," which proposed a cosmopolitan nationalism based on difference rather than a unified—and dangerous—Americanism, critic Randolph Bourne noted that Anglo Saxons blamed the war for stirring up ethnic feeling among immigrants. However, the dominant culture then "discovered with a moral shock that these movements had been making great headway before the war began. We found that the tendency, reprehensible and paradoxical as it might be, has been for the national clusters of immigrants, as they become more and more firmly established and more and more prosperous, to cultivate more and more assiduously the literatures and cultural traditions of their homeland."[7] This was the case within the Norwegian-American community, a situation that the immigrants both cultivated and widely debated. This dialogue would be ritualized in the 1925 Centennial, which was steeped in tensions over ethnic identity and Americanization.

The Centennial was a specific site of contestation that cannot be understood without first understanding these earlier debates and tensions. This chapter will examine the parameters of this debate within the community itself and in the larger and longer-range context of American nativism. As the previous chapter demonstrated, from at least the 1870s, families, workers, farmers, politicians, church leaders, and members of ethnic organizations were all involved in both private and public dialogues over language, politics, education, and Americanization in general. Artists, intellectuals, and journalists aired these debates before a wider audience in their novels, essays, and articles. In the context of nativism during World War I and the Red Scare, these debates became more heated and infused with a powerful new immediacy. The American schoolteacher, Hazel Knapp, the Houghlums, and their creator Rolvaag were all participants in the dialogue.

Rolvaag's concept of a pluralism that sustained and nurtured ethnic identities was shared by other ethnic intellectuals, as was his view of World War I as a major crisis for the cause of ethnic preservation. For example, Horace Kallen—known as the originator of the term "cultural pluralism"—vividly critiqued what he termed "Americanism" and its intensified forms during and after World War I. His works on cultural plural-ism began in 1914 and were published in the Norwegian-language press.[8] "The Great War," he wrote, "with its tanks and planes and poison gas has been followed by a battle of values, of norms, of standards; a struggle of theories of life. And it was the Great War which brought the battle on." In Kallen's view, the war transformed "the growing uneasiness of the native-born in the presence of the immigrant from an unconscious strain to a conscious repulsion, the condescending certainty of native superiority into an alarmed proclamation of it, and the naive assurance that it cannot be otherwise into a frenzied argument that it must be sheltered to survive."[9]

These intellectuals were responding to specific sociopolitical conditions. In 1914, the Leo Frank case, in which a northern Jewish industrialist was hung by vigilantes for the murder of a young Atlanta girl, incited a hysteri-cal anti-Semitism that reached national proportions.[10] A leaflet directed against blacks and Jews, signifying an important collapsing of categories, circulated in San Francisco: "Mr. White American, if you have any race pride or patriotism, you will organize for the protection of your race."[11] By 1917, Theodore Roosevelt advised Americans to shoot or hang any Ger-man they suspected of disloyalty. In April 1918, miners in southern Illinois lynched nineteen-year-old German immigrant Robert Prager.[12]

This kind of grassroots vigilantism was supported from above by groups like the American Protective League, a voluntary organization approved by the national government that reported on such things as "seditious and disloyal utterances." In 1918 the governor of Iowa banned any language except English in all public places and over the telephone. Other states followed with similar proclamations. After the war, a wave of class conflict led to the Palmer raids and the deportation of hundreds of immigrants, in-cluding the anarchist and revolutionary Emma Goldman. In August 1920, hundreds of immigrants and their children evacuated their homes in West Frankfort, Illinois, where for three days mobs burned homes and clubbed and stoned "foreigners."[13] In 1924 Congress passed the Immigration Re-striction Act, containing the most sweeping restrictions to date (immigra-tion would be restricted to 2 percent of each nationality present in 1890; the act excluded Asians, who were legally ineligible for citizenship). This was the national context within which Rolvaag and Kallen wrote.

Whatever particular groups had suffered at the hands of nativism be-fore—usually southern and eastern Europeans, Asians, and blacks—World War I and the years following saw an indiscriminate fear and distrust of foreigners in general. From the eugenics movement, racist anthropology, and race suicide theories of the elite to popular uprisings and vigilantism, all "hyphenates" posed a threat and needed to be contained, either through violence or the more subtle, "progressive" form of containment—assimilation. As a novel like *Pure Gold* demonstrates, the Norwegian Americans, like other "hyphenates," were deeply touched by these events, though certainly in less openly violent ways.

Politics, ethnic organization, religion, language, literature—all were part of a continuing discourse on ethnicity and assimilation in the Norwegian-American community before World War I, a discourse that grew more strident and immediate as America entered the war and nativism grew to a hysterical pitch. As Higham points out, World War I saw the "most strenuous nationalism and the most pervasive nativism that the United States had ever known." Germans were, of course, the first obvious target of war nativism, particularly when they openly rallied for U.S. neutrality early in the conflict. German Americans formed the largest group of foreign born in America and they had also been one of the most respected. The strong anti-German nativism was, according to Higham, a "spectacular reversal of judgment." But it was also part of a larger history of nativism and it is not surprising that a more vague anti-hyphenism grew out of specific anti-German feeling. The war years gave rise to a new expression—"100% Americanism," which "belligerently demanded universal conformity organized through total national loyalty." In this climate, passive assent was not enough. Americanism had to "be grasped and carried forward with evangelical fervor."[14] One is reminded here of Hazel Knapp and her blind patriotism bordering on violence. In this context, as Hazel well knew, dual identification with another nation was considered blasphemy and the loyalty of any "hyphenated" American was immediately called into question.

Norwegian Americans were not immune to the new "anti-hyphenism" for many reasons, not least of which was their attitude toward the war as it was generally perceived in the press. In the years immediately leading up to American intervention in 1917, the Norwegian-American press vacillated between pro-Ally and pro-German sentiments. Norway itself was neutral, and this was not lost on anti-hyphenists. More significant for outside opinion, however, were the votes on wartime resolutions in Congress. In February and March 1916, Congress acted on the Gore-McLemore resolutions, which advised Americans not to travel on belligerent ships. It was hoped that such resolutions would ensure continued U.S. neutrality. The resolutions were defeated, but eight of nine Norwegian Americans voting supported them. Conservative Senator Knute Nelson cast the only dissenting vote. An editorial in the *New York Times* attacked this Minnesota vote specifically: "The Minnesota delegation in Congress consists of eleven

Kaiserists and one American, and a mighty fine one, Senator Knute Nelson, born in Norway. . . . Knute Nelson is the only man, the sole American, Minnesota has in Congress."[15]

In April 1917, Congress voted on Wilson's declaration of war, which passed 82 to 6 in the Senate and 373 to 50 in the House. But only four of ten "Norwegian" votes were cast in support of Wilson. Those who voted against the resolution consistently referred to the war as merely a capitalist venture. For example, Senator John Nelson argued that industrialists supported the war for obvious reasons: "Is it not human nature that . . . bankers who have loaned billions to one side, or manufacturers of war materials who have sold billions of dollars' worth of munitions to one side, desire to see that side win with whom they have cast their lot?" More melodramatically, Congressman Harry Helgesen from North Dakota believed that the United States supported the Allies because so large a number of corporations "have been converted into factories for the production of munitions of war for Russia, France, and England. . . . [Therefore] our steel companies, our powder manufacturers and our makers of death-dealing instruments are reaping a fabulous harvest of wealth from this iniquitous traffic in human lives." A later study demonstrated that these Congressional feelings were shared by many Norwegian Americans. In a 1939 WPA survey in North Dakota, interviewers asked 121 first-generation Norwegian Americans if they had supported American intervention. Of these, 105 said no, 16 yes. One responded characteristically: "Did I favor American going into the first World War? No, I should say not, because I had the same idea then as now, only I did not dare say it then. We were fighting for the capitalists. They thought the Allies were going to lose the war; and they wanted Uncle Sam to go over and help, so they could collect what they had loaned—it was a money-man's war."[16] While such attitudes toward the war may perhaps be viewed less as ethnic than as concomitant with progressive politics, Americanizers in the English-language press and within the Norwegian-American community viewed such opposition as a sign of disloyalty and a result of "hyphenism." Though many "dared not say it then," the negative attitudes of many Norwegian Americans toward the war—in addition to their numbers in radical labor and farmer politics—were well known and created an "image" problem for the whole community.[17]

In addition to this opposition to the war, Norwegian Americans had been vulnerable to attacks by anti-hyphenists because of their continued use of the Norwegian language, their strong immigrant press, and their thriving ethnic organizations. Both Theodore Roosevelt and Woodrow Wilson launched attacks on such activities at least two years before war was declared. In 1915 Roosevelt told a gathering of the Knights of Columbus,

> During the last year and a quarter it has been brought home to us in startling fashion that many of the elements of our nation are not yet properly fused. . . . The one absolutely certain way of bringing this nation to ruin . . . would be to permit it to become a tangle of squabbling nationalities . . . each preserving its separate nationality, each at heart feeling more sympathy with Europeans of that nationality than with others of the American Republic. The men who do not become Americans and nothing else are hyphenated Americans; and there ought to be no room for them in this country.[18]

Earlier that same year, Wilson had spoken with a bit more restraint—but perhaps with more covert threat—to an audience of recently naturalized immigrants: "And while you bring all countries with you, you come with a purpose of leaving all other countries behind you—bringing what is best of their spirit, but not looking over your shoulders and seeking to perpetuate what you intended to leave behind in them . . . you cannot become thorough Americans if you think of yourselves in groups. America does not consist of groups. A man who thinks of himself as belonging to a particular national group in America has not yet become an American."[19] Both Roosevelt's and Wilson's statements called not only for political loyalty but, if taken literally, for cultural loyalty as well. Such a demand made all ethnic activity suspect.

Wilson's address in particular sparked a long and heated discussion of hyphenism in the Norwegian-American community. Some felt that Wilson's speech and the anti-hyphenist movement posed no direct threat; some, like Senator Knute Nelson, joined the movement, and others perceived a "clear and present danger" to Norwegian-American identity.[20] The debate, as analyzed by Carl Chrislock, centered specifically around whether Wilson was actually asking for cultural loyalty as well as political loyalty. All agreed that if he was, he had no right to do so. In a direct response to Wilson's address, a *Fram* editorial argued that "Yankee blue bloods" did not need to question immigrant loyalty if the United States entered the war, for immigrants had always fought loyally in American conflicts. Another paper, the *Fergus Falls Ugeblad*, viewed Wilson's speech as a direct attack, stating that the "vast majority of hyphenated Americans are among the best citizens of the land," who should be allowed—and encouraged—to maintain "their hyphen." In addition to this direct threat from national policy figures, Norwegians could point to local attacks on their ethnicity. In 1915 the *Minneapolis Journal* published an editorial titled

"The Hyphen Must Go!" The editorial contended that the melting pot was not doing its job in the upper Midwest. Immigrant communities were retaining too much of their Old World culture and too many "hyphenated" newspapers, schools, and societies were still using their native languages.[21]

Such attacks led to a larger deliberation on anti-hyphenism in general. For example, in a letter to *Fram* in 1915, North Dakota author Simon Johnson argued that the term "hyphenated Americanism" was a derogatory characterization not in keeping with American democracy. According to Johnson, instead of being reshaped into perfect Americans—which he found impossible anyway—immigrants should cultivate inherited values that would enrich American culture.[22] Similarly, *bygdelag* leaders "commented upon" and "used" Horace Kallen's concept of cultural pluralism to defend their existence. Knut Lokensgaard, president of Hallinglaget from 1918 to 1925, argued that in order to be truly American, ethnics must "cultivate" their heritage, which would "benefit" the whole nation.[23] Throughout 1915 and 1916, Ager dedicated many editorial pages in *Reform* and essays in *Kvartalskrift* to such "pro-hyphenist" arguments. Chrislock points out that one recurring theme in these pieces was that a "strong political motivation underlay the campaign to annihilate the hyphen."[24] For instance, Ager contended that if all ethnic differences disappeared, then the Anglo-Americans would achieve true political hegemony. In his longer essays, he argued against the "melting pot." In the most literal use of this term, Henry Ford had his workers stage a pageant in which immigrants in their native dress and speaking their native language walked into a giant cauldron, emerging again as "100%" Americans in red, white, and blue costumes, holding American flags. In Ager's preservationist view, "the melting pot does not produce good citizens, nor does it produce anything else that is good, unless one cherishes a definitely low and common standard as normal for everybody." Ager believed that "pure" ethnicity was the only answer. "The Norwegian who became a good citizen in Norway and became just as good a citizen in this country will also become a good and useful citizen in Canada if he settles there."[25] In other words, Norwegian culture should be a welcomed and respected addition to American society and should not be subjected to any mixing or melting.

Ager's views were rebutted in other newspapers as well as in his own journal. Interestingly, in many of these rebuttals, Ager's preservationism was attacked primarily on the grounds of his opposition to the war. For example, one of his strongest adversaries was Rasmus Bjorn Anderson, who in 1915 attached the slogan "My Country Right or Wrong" to the masthead of his weekly Norwegian-language newspaper, *Amerika*. Anderson argued that the attack on hyphens had nothing to do with cultural activities, only political loyalty—which of course should be given without question. Likewise, the newspaper *Normanden* called for complete support of Roosevelt and Wilson, arguing vehemently against the pro-hyphenist views of at least three Norwegian-language journals, including Ager's. Like Anderson, the *Normanden* editors did not perceive any threat against immigrant cultural activities, only a rightful call to political allegiance.[26] Indeed, the only threat came from those "hyphens" who opposed the war. In response to such statements, Ager wrote in 1917: "We are Americans in the sense that we feel this to be our country, the flag our flag, and our interests identical with the interests of the nation. We are Americans to the extent that we wish to live in this country and for the country, and if need be to die for it. This is the way we should be and must be, if we are to take our citizenship seriously. . . . It is a question of honesty, loyalty, and a sense of duty. However, if we do not possess these qualities as Norwegian-Americans, we certainly cannot acquire them by changing name, and language, and clothes, and religion.' "[27] Ager perceived more acutely than the others that a call to cultural conformity was submerged under the seemingly legitimate call for political loyalty.

When Wilson declared war on Germany, this controversy over hyphenism turned into a debate about specific ethnic activities and whether they should be curtailed during wartime. Like the arguments about hyphenism, this debate centered on whether ethnic festivals constituted a breach of political loyalty, bespeaking the crucial links between politics and culture. In 1917 three Norwegian-language newspapers printed an anonymous proposal from a "prominent" Norwegian American. The author suggested that Norwegian Americans curtail May 17 festivals celebrating the signing of the Norwegian constitution in 1814. The three editors who printed the letter agreed. Several smaller papers responded with vehement disagreement. For example, *Normanden* printed the following: "If our departed fathers, who bequeathed us a worthy heritage, could hear the nonsense now being disseminated in the name of loyalty, they undoubtedly would turn over in their graves. If the distinguished editors, who in this instance give the impression of speaking for thousands of human beings, already have lost their senses, what will happen when the nation confronts a really serious crisis? Presumably, they will then admonish Norwegian Americans to refrain from speaking Norwegian even in the intimate setting of an evening by the fireside."[28] It seems that the editors at *Normanden* were beginning to sense what Ager had known all along. May 17 festivities went on as scheduled throughout the war, though with a new theme of American patriotism as camouflage. Indeed, the anxiety and tension implicit in the discussion speak more to the larger political climate than to the specific argument over ethnic festivals.

For the anxiety expressed here was heightened by sociopolitical activity that led an author such as Rolvaag to term this period "The Day of the Great Beast." Nationwide nativist activities were covered in Norwegian-language papers and drew characteristic response from Ager. For example, in 1917, Ager commented on an increase in violence against blacks in Texas, making a connection with general nativism and collapsing the crucial differences between racial violence against blacks and nativistic violence against "hyphenates." He wrote, "The racial confrontation in Houston reminds us again of our unresolved domestic problems. In East St. Louis and other places, whites have massacred Negroes. The Negro soldiers, who are preparing to embark for France to fight for us, deserve some guarantee that their wives, parents, and children will not be victims of race hatred in this country while they are fighting for democracy in Europe."[29] The "unresolved domestic problem" of "race hatred" surely seemed even more immediate when Norwegian Americans learned of vicious attacks on German Americans. Rolvaag's reference to lynching in *Pure Gold* attests to this fear of violence on the part of all minorities during World War I.

Nativism touched the Norwegian Americans directly in less physically violent ways, though the cultural violence was powerful. For example, an alien registration bill was put into effect by the Minnesota Commission on Public Safety, an agency created by the 1917 legislature. The commission, modeled on the national agency, was created to respond to two perceived threats within the state: a large population of immigrants and their children, and a growing radical movement on the Iron Range and among Nonpartisan Leaguers, many of whom were Scandinavian. Many made an explicit connection between these two threats, linking "hyphenates" to radical politics. To deal with the possible disloyalty of immigrants in general, the MCPS Women's Auxiliary Committee, chaired by Alice Ames Winter, launched a full-scale Americanization campaign in fifty-six counties, aimed at teaching English, patriotism, and Americanism. In 1918 Winter declared, "Before the impetus of war is lost, we must be sure that we have set in motion forces that will Americanize every foreigner in our midst. EVERY COUNTY SHOULD HAVE A PERMANENT AMERICANIZATION COMMITTEE."[30]

As one way to energize immigrant patriotism, the Commission appointed Nicolay Grevstad, a Norwegian American, to monitor immigrant-language newspapers and institutions. Grevstad wrote that a strong educational campaign was urgently needed among the Scandinavian-Americans, who were prone to more left-wing ideas about the war. The campaign, according to Grevstad, should "correct misinformation, supply needed information, repress disloyalty where it may be found, and . . . convert passive loyalty into wholehearted, strong, and active support of the administration and its war measures."[31] On a national level, Congress instituted regulations aimed at the foreign-language press. Editors were required to file with the postmaster translations of any article dealing with the war or government policy. The only way to avoid this was to secure a presidential exemption, which was given to Scandinavian-language newspapers that were endorsed by Senator Knute Nelson and Grevstad. Publications that leaned more to the left were required to file translations.

This fear of immigrant disloyalty kept hidden by a foreign language culminated in governmental moves to curtail foreign-language use altogether. In 1918, for example, Governor Harding of Iowa issued his wartime language proclamation calling for the use of English in all public places, including over the telephone. At least fifteen other governors legislated similar restrictions. Harding argued that continued use of foreign languages created discord at a time when the country desperately required unity. He hoped that his proclamation would "result in peace and tranquillity at home and greatly strengthen the country in battle."[32] No one in the Norwegian-American press or leadership approved of Harding's proposal, but criticism varied. Some viewed it as a direct outgrowth of hysterical anti-hyphenism. One woman wrote to the governor, accusing him of combating " 'Prussianism in Europe and [practicing] it in the homeland.' " The Sons of Norway issued a strong condemnation of the edict. They sent Harding a resolution protesting " 'unwarranted and unlawful attempts to curtail the rights and liberties of free, loyal, American citizens.' "[33] Others, like Senator Nelson, agreed that the governor had gone too far, but his call for complete loyalty was necessary. Harding's proclamation was only the most famous of many local demands for a decreased use of foreign languages in schools, newspapers, and churches.

The Norwegian Lutheran churches found themselves in the midst of this controversy. The church faced problems in addition to its continued use of Norwegian in many of its services and its ongoing theological struggles. In 1917 the *Lutheranen* commented that "everyone knows that the Lutheran church originated in Germany and this does not enhance its popularity here in America at the present time.' "[34] The church was in the paradoxical position of needing to assert its separateness from German Lutherans—and hence its loyalty to America—at the same time that it was in the process of merging the various synods into one Norwegian Lutheran organization. Merger had long been an issue among the various synods, but theological and political differences militated against it. After 1900, however, as Norwegian Americans grew more urbanized and the new wave of immigrants were likewise from more urban areas, it became increasingly clear that the various synods were losing power in the community, a power and influence that merger might restore. To a new generation less concerned with old theological controversies, a unified church offered an appeal on larger ethnic grounds.

The merger took place in 1917, resulting in a synod of 3,276 congregations, 1,054 pastors, and a half million members.[35] Merging and consolidation, a move taken by many immigrant churches in the early twentieth century, not only allowed for a more centralized authority, but also increased resources. And, united, the Lutheran church would maintain its leadership role in ethnic solidarity. Indeed, Missouri Synod leaders criticized the merger as less religious than nationalistic. (This is an interesting accusation given the tendency of German immigrants to merge "symbols of religion and nationalism" in Missouri Synod congregations.)[36] E. Clifford Nelson has described the ways in which nationalism was a factor in unification. First, social groups like the *bygdelag*, based on localized ties in Norway, cut across religious lines and drew immigrants together in a way that militated against separate congregations. Second, he points out that all synods were "bound together by a common *Norwegian* version of Lutheran hymnody and catechetical instruction." And third, the church leaders themselves often argued for unification based on nationalistic grounds. The most obvious indication of this was the choice for the name of the church. Rather than "The United Lutheran Synod in America," one of the proposals, leaders chose "The Norwegian Lutheran Church of America."[37]

The NLCA began in a very contradictory and tenuous position. On the one hand, it appealed to ethnic solidarity in a climate of intense hostility. On the other hand, in the context of that climate, it had to prove its loyalty to the larger American society. As Nelson put it, "Janus-like, the church which emerged in 1917 faced in two directions: towards the past from which it had received its heritage, and towards the future which might easily erode its heritage."[38] In part to set themselves off from any taint of "Germanness," the NLCA involved itself in several war-related activities, including Liberty Bond promotions and other fund-raising drives. Despite these efforts, questions about Lutheran patriotism continued. In 1918 a Department of Justice official warned the Minnesota Commission on Public Safety: "You are advised that disloyalty is quite a common fault among

Ministers of the Luthern [sic] Church."[39] At the same time, Senator Knute Nelson called for a much more powerful patriotic role for the churches. The NLCA in response endorsed a "Patriotic Plea," asking that the clergy actively support the war directly from the pulpit.

This in turn raised questions about the very name of the church. "Norwegian" as a designator seemed to undermine the church's claim to political loyalty. At its biennial convention in 1918, church leaders voted 533 to 61 to remove the word "Norwegian" from the NLCA's name and appointed a committee to prepare a resolution for the next constitutional convention. The Synod president's report justified the decision: "Since our country entered the war, a great reversal has taken place in the direction of rapid assimilation." Opponents of the resolution accused proponents of giving into the anxiety fostered by Governor Harding's language edict. One claimed that "the killing poison gas of the war spirit was strongly in evidence."[40] The name change caused an outcry in the community. The church had been one of the primary institutions to stand for ethnic identity in the community; the loss of "Norwegian" as a designator signaled a loss of Norwegian-American culture in general. The act thus became a magnet for all the anxieties and conflicts over the anti-hyphenist movement and wartime hysteria.

Four years later, Rolvaag addressed the role of the church in the Norwegian community in the last chapter of *Omkring Faedrearven (Reflections on Our Heritage)*. He believed that the church should play a central role in fostering Norwegian-American identity rather than join with larger English-speaking synods. He wrote: "Of course we are Americans, and nothing but Americans—as citizens! Whatever else should we be? . . . But by descent, by origin, by family, we are Norwegians, and can never be anything else no matter how desperately some of us try. . . . I believe that it remains the church's unalterable duty to take advantage of this fact. If it does so, I believe that there are laid up for us riches and possibilities that we have scarcely touched as yet." He finished his book, a lengthy plea to the Norwegian-American community, with the following statement: "That is enough. Nevertheless, it is difficult to put the final period on paper when one begins to write about these things. . . . And never has there been greater confusion in our thinking than just at this time."[41]

The end of the war seemed to matter little in this confusion—both in terms of the national nativist movement which continued well into the 1920s and in terms of the ongoing controversies and debates within the Norwegian-American community. The response of the community to wartime nativism was a resurgence of ethnic activity, including the enormous success of a Norwegian-American literature that confronted issues of ethnicity, Americanization, and nativism; in 1920, the lay membership of the church managed to reinstate, at least for a time, the word "Norwegian" in the NLCA; ethnic organizations and historical societies were revitalized and created anew as a direct reaction to nativism and the growing restrictionist movement. The 1925 Immigration Centennial was a direct outgrowth of this activity. As John Bodnar points out, such a response was not unusual. During and after the war, "growing federal power and the consequent stress on patriotism and civic duty had a distinct impact on local commemorations in ethnic communities, cities, states, and regions." As "official" expressions of loyalty and patriotism attempted to displace immigrant and local conceptions of history and identity, "subcultures" responded creatively "in a valiant attempt to preserve something of their own interests."[42]

Despite such activity, Norwegian language-use did decline in these years and ethnic institutions deteriorated to some degree, particularly after 1925. Hence, historians of the Norwegian-American experience most often end their narratives with this date—Norwegian-American ethnicity is essentially over by 1925.

Because the subtext of these narratives is often a belief in assimilation as a "natural" process, these historians read their evidence in a way that reflects this belief. According to this view, Norwegian-American history progressed through a stage of ethnic strength and solidarity into a crisis wrought by hegemonic nativism. The Norwegian Americans responded with a brief flourish of ethnicity, but in every vital sense they were moving inevitably toward assimilation. But if we acknowledge that assimilation is a constructed narrative, predicated on deep anxieties about the Other, we should be compelled to reread that evidence. Rather than hastening Americanization, World War I nativism heated and made more immediate a dialogue in the Norwegian-American community that had been going on for many years. Norwegian-American culture up to World War I was not a "transitional" bridge from a vital Norwegianess to full Americanism. At no time was there an "authentic" Norwegian-American culture that was replaced by American culture. As the debates within families, institutions, in literature, and in the press demonstrate, ethnic identity was continually contested and negotiated. Threats from within and without were ever present. The Hazel Knapps and the children hiding in the cornfield to speak Norwegian were all making real historical choices and participating in real historical struggles. A static and finite view of ethnicity distorts these choices and struggles. Neither the Americanization movement nor the Norwegian-American response to it was a direct product of the war. Both had a much longer and more complex history than this standard view suggests.

This period in Norwegian-American history demonstrates that tensions over Americanization were resolved in favor of neither assimilation nor ethnic maintenance, though both continued to be possibilities. Rather, these issues continued to be contested and would be encoded and ritualized in the centennial celebration of 1925. The next chapter will explore the ways in which the Centennial's middle-class organizers constructed a narrative of Norwegian-American history that masked the many tensions and debates about ethnicity in their community. Their conservative vision was an effort to both regain and maintain their positions as leaders in a viable ethnic community and to present their values to the larger culture as compatible with American culture, business, and politics.

4

"The Pride of the Race Had Been Touched": Constructing a Festival Identity

✦✦✦✦✦✦

On June 5, 1925, seventy-five thousand Norwegian Americans listened to President Calvin Coolidge praise Norwegian contributions to America. Coolidge even acknowledged their claim that a Norwegian explorer actually discovered America long before Columbus. A local journalist reported the crowd's response: "The great roar that rose from Nordic throats to Thor and Odin above the lowering gray clouds told that the pride of the race had been touched."[1] As a preamble to this main event, five hundred Norwegian-American schoolchildren, draped in red, white, and blue capes, stood arranged as the flag of Norway. Their rendition of the "familiar and beloved" Norwegian national anthem met with "a din of applause and cheers of approval." Before the applause died down, the children transformed themselves into the image of the American flag, followed by "The Star-Spangled Banner" and the audience's continued shouts and cheering. In her later account of the spectacle, Mrs. John O. Lee argued that all those who viewed the "living flag" were "the better men and women, the better Americans for having witnessed it." In Lee's view, the transformation out of "apparent temporary chaos" signified a more important transformation. "For in what more strikingly forceful manner could be visualized the ease and willingness with which the immigrants have ever become American citizens? . . . It epitomized as nothing else did or could the underlying thought of the Norse-American Centennial."[2]

This dual celebration of Norwegian and American nationalisms indeed epitomized in many ways the vision of the men and women who organized the Centennial. But if the main goal was to "visualize the ease and willingness" of Norwegian assimilation to American life, the celebration of Norwegian nationalism would have been superfluous. In another statement about the two flags, a second Norwegian-American woman noted that the colors of the two signify the same values and beliefs: courage, freedom, truth, justice, and democracy. It was, therefore, not "unfitting to blend them in harmonious consecration. . . ."[3] In nearly every aspect of the Centennial celebration, organizers wanted to portray a particular image about Norwegian Americans—that they had easily become American citizens because, as Norwegians and descendants of Norwegians, they innately possessed American ideals. Indeed, in the souvenir program, Professor O. M. Norlie asserted that the Anglo-Saxon ancestors of dominant culture Americans were very closely related to Norwegians. In fact, he argues, the English, Irish, and French counties who witnessed the most emigration to America were once ruled by Norwegians—"the Pilgrim Fathers themselves were mainly of Norwegian descent."[4]

At the same time that traditional signifiers of ethnicity such as ethnic institutions and language-use were on the wane, the middle-class organizers of the Centennial constructed an ethnic identity that placed their community at the center of forming a democratic, American society. Sold and presented to its audience with a boosterism that rivaled George Babbitt's talents, the organizers' vision of their ethnicity served some very specific political and class interests. Utilizing a secular jeremiad form prevalent in Progressive-Era civic celebrations, the organizers hoped to combat threats to the ethnic community from both within and without. In constructing their narrative, organizers made concrete choices about what and whom to include and to exclude, choices which worked to promote a particular kind of Norwegian Americaness. In the context of an eroding ethnic enclave, these organizers wanted to strengthen and preserve their positions as leaders in an ethnic community. At the same time, in an era of tremendous conservatism and pressure to conform, they constructed a narrative through specific representations of their history that signified Norwegian-American ethnicity in the 1920s as "safe" for American politics, business, and culture.

In his important work on invented traditions, Eric Hobsbawm argues that in times of rapid change and social dislocation, people invent traditions that make ritualized connections to the past and promote group identity and solidarity by inculcating "appropriate" values and behaviors.[5] The traditions are meant to unify the group despite differences between potential members. Historians who have recently begun to investigate invented traditions in ethnic cultures have found that in times of crisis, the "symbolic umbrella of the ethnic culture" served "several, often contradictory, purposes." The symbols, rituals, and slogans must provide a sense of solidarity among disparate members of the ethnic community.

Fig. 7: President Calvin Coolidge and the first lady arrive for the festivities at the fairgrounds grandstand. *Courtesy Minnesota Historical Society.*

Fig. 8: Schoolchildren posed in the Norwegian formation of the "Living Flag". *Courtesy Minnesota Historical Society.*

The group is then mobilized to "defend its cultural values and to advance its claims to power, status, and resources." At the same time, paradoxically, the purpose of this "symbolic umbrella" is to defuse the hostility of the larger culture by claiming a compatibility with American values and ideals.[6] Likewise, John Bodnar, in his study of twentieth-century public memory, argues that "public memory emerges from the intersection of official and vernacular cultural expressions." The "official" view is rooted "in the concerns of cultural leaders or authorities at all levels of society." Those authorities could be national government officials, town authorities, or ethnic community leaders. What they all have in common is "an interest in social unity, the continuity of existing institutions, and loyalty to the status quo."[7] The tensions and contradictions of such an effort may also bespeak a challenge to American values and ideals, but the overt creation of this "symbolic umbrella" is a useful model for understanding the Centennial organizers' efforts and goals in formulating and carrying out the celebration.

The Centennial effort began in 1920, when a joint council of *bygdelag*, called *Bygdelagenes Fellesraad*, passed a resolution to organize an immigration celebration. The joint council was formed in 1917, following the *bygdelag's* decision in 1914 that they should continue to cooperate in organizing festivals after the success of the Eidsvoll celebration. Following the trend during World War I, the council held few meetings but began to organize in earnest in 1920. In addition to voting on the Centennial resolution, the 1920 meeting reaffirmed a 1919 committee formed to "guard against" legislative attempts to forbid the use of the Norwegian language in public forums. According to *bygdelag* historian Odd Lovoll, World War I Americanism had taken by surprise those who spoke strongly for the preservation of Norwegian culture. By the 1920 meeting, "They were ready to launch a counter-offensive in order to retain precious features of their national tradition."[8]

Though the *bygdelag* connotes "folk" origins, by 1924 the Centennial was being organized by a committee made up largely of members of the professional and business class whose purpose went well beyond cultural preservation. In November 1923, the council elected officers authorized to organize the Centennial. Gisle Bothne, professor of Scandinavian Studies at the University of Minnesota and president of *Smallalenslaget*, was elected president. Before the association was incorporated in 1924, great care was given to choosing executive officers. For example, State Representative N. T. Moen wrote to S. H. Holstad concerning the choice of a president: he should be a man who is "able to talk and write in both languages; he should have quite a recognized standing among our people, the Norse Element, and be looked upon with special recognition by our 'Lag' and 'Church People.' "⁹ In the end, the officers included an impressive list of the community's elite. Bothne continued as president; Moen, also president of *Osterdalslaget,* was appointed vice president; managing director S. H. Holstad owned S. H. Holstad Coffee Company; J. A. Holvik, a professor at Concordia College, acted as secretary; chairman of the committee on exhibits, Knut Gjerset, was curator of the Norwegian pioneer museum in Decorah, Iowa; secretary of the Women's Auxiliary of the Executive Committee, Caroline Storlie, was a member of several Scandinavian organizations, a member of the State Central Committee of the Democratic Party in 1922, and an active member of the National Woman's Party; and chairman of the Finance Committee, E. G. Quamme, was president of the Federal Land Bank in St. Paul. Eventually, honorary members of the executive committee would include governors from states with large Norwegian populations, more prominent businessmen and a few prominent women—usually teachers—and senators, congressmen, and college presidents of Norwegian descent. The committee incorporated in July 1924, raising capital by selling stock and taking gifts and loans from the *bygdelag*. The *Bygdelagenes Fellesraad* turned over control of the administration to what was now called Norse-American Centennial, Incorporated.

Headquartered in Minneapolis, the Centennial committee oversaw a massive national organization of committees with over four thousand members. The committee appointed a male and female chair from each state, who first located Norwegian Americans residing in that state, a negligible number in some cases. Female chairs in places like Texas and Kansas showed a great interest in the Centennial, but were continually frustrated in their efforts to locate Norwegian Americans in their states. Judith Jacobs wrote to publicity director Oscar Arneson in April 1925, that "the Kansas situation is correctly described by Rev. Hjarthohn. He says, 'To look for Norse people in Kansas is about like looking for a needle in a haystack.' "¹⁰ But she assured Arneson that they would keep trying. Following this original census of sorts, forty-two states were organized to a greater or lesser degree. The chair, Caroline Storlie, then appointed county and township chairs—all women—who oversaw ticket sales, collected exhibit materials, and promoted the celebration through educational programs. Such organization resulted in the largest nationwide festival celebrating Norwegian immigration.

According to David Glassberg, the overt purpose of many American festivals in the Progressive Era, even when they incorporated elements of ethnic "folk" activities, was to assimilate immigrants into the dominant American traditions. This became even more pronounced in the nativistic climate of World War I; festivals then focused on strictly American traditions.[11] Civic officials used historical imagery in celebrations to "forge a public historical consciousness from a multiplicity of available traditions and images. . . ." Civic officials elicited public participation by constructing a history that was "shaped by popular expectations as well as civic officials' political agenda and power." Glassberg found that "from the perspective of the organizers," what unified the celebration and "by extension" the participants, was a "central historical theme" that was carried through the orations, the decorations, the music, the processions, and the pageants. "Set like a sermon amid a religious program of invocations, hymns, and benedictions, the historical oration narrated the lessons of local and national history in a civil-religious format that suggested sacred as well as worldly significance." Speakers used a secular jeremiad format, connecting past and future into a glorious transcendence of present troubles, linking "national moral ideals and the concrete details of local material progress."[12]

In very similar ways, the organizers of the Norse-American Centennial presented a grand historical narrative whose purpose was to unite Norwegian Americans to a heroic past in order to meet better the demands of a culture which sought to obliterate difference. Organizers were conscious of the similarity between their celebration and American festivities in the same period. They made repeated references to the Mayflower celebration of 1920, and Oscar Olson, a member of the Centennial committee of Luther College, urged organizers to make a "careful survey" of all expositions and celebrations that had been held in America in recent years. Such a "worthy" celebration, Olson prophesied, would allow Norwegian Americans to "secure a better understanding of their heritage, a better appreciation of their pioneer fathers, a more just recognition by their American neighbors, and thus become better able to face the future. . . ."[13] Not only does Olson make an explicit connection to other celebrations, but he invokes the jeremiad form that Glassberg has found so prevalent in American celebrations.

These rhetorical strategies point to the overtly conservative nature of the celebration. Implicit in Olson's statement and in the celebration's narrative was the belief that Norwegian Americans must overcome a threat from both without and within—from nativists who wanted to dissolve any differences among Americans and from a younger generation of Norwegian Americans who no longer appreciated its "heritage." By the 1920s, the

growth of a modern capitalist system that encouraged individual autonomy and pleasure through consumption seriously undermined communal
bonds in many different areas of life, from voluntary associations to ethnic
enclaves. While Norwegian Americans were among those who benefited
from modern capitalism and the new consumer culture, the institutions
and values of both threatened the communal ties that continued to exist in
the community. Many Norwegian Americans joined others in the early
flight to the suburbs, away from urban ethnic enclaves.[14] These urban
areas, particularly in New York, Chicago, Minneapolis, and Seattle, where
Norwegian ethnic neighborhoods were the sites of substantial ethnic businesses and institutions, gave rise to an ethnic elite "who dominated the
public life of the *koloni* [neighborhood] and claimed to represent the group
in its dealings outside the neighborhood."[15] Suburbanization proved a
paradox for such ethnic elites. On the one hand, ethnic newspapers in the
1920s championed home ownership as proof that Norwegians were loyal
Americans. On the other hand, flight from urban enclaves would certainly
weaken their hold on the community. The Sons of Norway lodge thrived in
the 1920s suburbs, but little else institutional did. And, like other young
Americans, whether in the city or the suburbs, Norwegian-American
youth participated in the new lifestyle of the consumer culture, shedding
"traditional" values and standards of behavior.

Lizbeth Cohen, however, has recently questioned our standard view of
the 1920s as a decade when a mass consumer culture served to homoge-
nize ethnic and working-class Americans. She has discovered that, even
when they did participate in the consumer culture, working-class ethnics
in Chicago did so within their communities and often interpreted consumer behavior very differently from the larger middle-class culture.[16]
John Jenswold points out that perhaps even a move to the suburbs connoted a rural tradition of home ownership among Norwegians.[17] What
appears to be part of a homogenizing mass culture, like a festival celebration, may have many different meanings attached to it.

In an opening-day lecture on immigration history in the early 1920s at
St. Olaf College, Rolvaag admonished his students for knowing neither the
Norwegian language nor the history of Norwegian settlement in America.
"So," he told them, "I am giving this course in the boyish hope that I
hereby may lead a few of our own young people to think more of their
fathers and mothers and the work they have done in this country, to appreciate their own race more. . . . Hence I am giving this course in the hope
that those who take it will become better Americans. For there is no true
patriotism possible unless it is built on the love of home and fireside." He

also wished to demonstrate to his students how much the Norwegians had materially contributed to the building of the Northwest. But he continued with a challenge: "Shall [we] do our full share in a spiritual way? That depends on you—the younger generation. You must press onward into the future with all possible energy." But also "you must show the greatest faithfulness to your race, to the cultural and spiritual heritage which you have received and which you may receive in still larger measure if you care. You must not erase your racial characteristics in order to become better Americans. You must deepen them if possible."[18]

Rolvaag was equally concerned about the older generation of Norwegian Americans, who, according to him, were also taking flight into the consumer culture and becoming increasingly disinterested in their ethnic community. In his forward to "Reflections on Our Heritage," from which he took his speech for the Centennial, he wrote that he hoped to "stimulate discussion and, even more, awake greater interest. It is interest we must arouse—first of all. Later on we can expect action. . . . The folk-soul is still healthy. If only we could set it aflame!"[19]

Rolvaag's concerns and challenges paralleled those of the Centennial organizers. For example, Ragna Grimsby, chairwoman for Montana and national organizer, wrote to the committee, "I have always cherished everything that savors of the Norwegian and miss the good old Norse ways of home. Out here very little Norse is spoken, and very little is known of Norwegian culture and literature, especially among the young people."[20] Mirroring Grimsby's concern, in the discussion among committee members about whether to use English or Norwegian as the official language of the Centennial, many felt it particularly necessary to advertise and correspond in English so that the younger generation would be sure to understand and grasp the full import of the event. And, like Grimsby, Rev. Jens Roseland of Pennsylvania was concerned about his ability to organize his state. He lamented to the committee, "Our Philadelphia Norsemen are a much-divided and slow-moving bunch. . . ."[21] The organizers' positions as leaders of a strong, viable ethnic community were in danger in this context. They attempted, in a prewar progressive style, to counteract the perceived disaffection of many Norwegian Americans and the moral lapses of the youth by revitalizing traditional "ethnic" values of home, family, and community.

At the same time, in order to maintain the prosperity they had achieved, the organizers also confronted the threat from outside the community. The threat of consumerism as a culturally homogenizing force was, as discussed in the previous chapter, only second to the continuing efforts by politicians, civic leaders, and, increasingly, "ordinary" citizens, to Americanize "hyphenated" citizens and limit immigration. Ironically, at the same time that ethnics like the Centennial organizers attempted to revitalize traditional values of home and family, the larger culture linked such communities to a generalized notion of foreigness and, therefore, to a radicalism that was a danger to American values and business. Wartime nativism intensified in the South and the Midwest in the form of an increasingly large membership in the Ku Klux Klan, which gained enormous political clout for its emphasis on "traditional" rural values and 100% Americanism. The nativism, however, was not limited to rural fundamentalists. Prewar reformers continued to battle for immigration restriction laws and the business classes urged a conformism that would smooth labor relations and pave the way to continued prosperity.[22] In a culture of consumption periodically interrupted by labor unrest, conformity was good business.

In Sinclair Lewis's satire of 1920s conformity, George Babbitt, a "substantial citizen," addresses the Zenith Real Estate Board on the virtues of "standardization," not only in goods and services, but in thought, values, and vocabulary. While Lewis's account is fictional, it brilliantly captures the era and dramatizes the context in which the Centennial organizers operated. The "Ideal Citizen" was a rational businessman who puts "zip into some store or profession or art." He is "a supporter of the hearthstone which is the basic foundation of our civilization. . . . Here's the new generation of Americans: fellows with hair on their chests and smiles in their eyes and adding-machines in their offices." When Babbitt later begins to doubt the efficacy of complete conformity, he comes under the watchful eye and overt threats of the Good Citizens' League, whose most "important" struggle was against union labor. The League fought unions in part through an Americanization drive "so that newly arrived foreigners might learn that the true-blue and one hundred per cent American way of settling labor-troubles was for workmen to love and trust their employers."[23]

In such a context, the organizers took great pains to promote the Centennial as a nonpolitical event, to unite various factions in the community under their own particular vision of Norwegian-American ethnicity. In January 1925, Director Holstad wrote to Minnesota Congressman O. J. Kvale, encouraging him to present the state legislature's resolution about the efficacy and worthiness of the Centennial to Secretary of State Kellogg, a Minnesota native known for his connections to big business and his conservative views about "hyphenated" Americans. Holstad wrote, "I know that 'fools rush in where angels fear to tread,' and I may be talking plain foolishness, [but] you know the celebration is non-political, non-religious, and 100% American."[24] As Bothne's humorous reference to Kellogg's politics suggests, this nonpolitical position was not unproblematic. That the organizers did not accept an Americanization model is clear from Congressman Knud Wefald's correspondence with Bothne about a bill in Congress aimed at a freer flow of travel between the United States and other countries. Wefald noted that "the jingo element in Congress always seizes on an occasion like this to make capital for themselves." He planned to undertake an amendment to a "vicious immigration law" passed in the previous session, noting that it was "high time that we resume the social and intellectual intercourse with Europe again, and that we do not look upon every foreigner as a criminal."[25] The narrative the organizers created, however, set them apart from more "suspect" foreigners. For their efforts, they received complete support from President Coolidge. In his speech at the fairgrounds, he declared, "Americans who admire the accomplishments of these hard-working, thrifty men and women of Norse blood that have made such splendid citizens must remember that under our immigration laws only 6,500 Norwegians may be admitted yearly. Congress, neglecting the country's need of a selective immigration policy which would let in the sort of Europeans the land most needs, put up bars against some of the most superior races."[26]

The Norwegian-American organizers accomplished such a favorable position through a process of historical reconstruction that posed a seamless narrative of Norwegian-American history. In April 1925, Holstad noted that "perhaps the word 'centennial' does not adequately express the nature of the gathering," though one aspect of the celebration was the commemoration of the immigrant sloop in 1825.[27] More than a centennial, it was a wide-ranging celebration of a specific Norwegian-American identity with roots in both the romantic tales of the Viking age and the pioneer immigration that resulted in a people peculiarly situated to contribute to a vital American democracy. In an essay printed in the souvenir program, O. M. Norlie asserted that those groups who have the most "inspiring" histories and are proud of those histories are those who have the "brightest future." Invoking the secular jeremiad form, Norlie argued,

> American history is mainly New England and accordingly New England has influenced America more than any other section or people. Norwegians could be more influential if their history were better known and if they themselves

stood up more stoutly for their ideals. The Norwegian Centennial should make it plain that they have a proud history, and it should inspire them to still nobler ideals. As Norwegian Americans we should be able to face the future with a new pride, faith, and prayer.

These ideals in which the Norwegians should pride themselves were numerous, from being "foremost" in farming, literacy, lawfulness, and religious spirituality to their many cultural "brothers" who had made a name for Norwegians in American politics, literature, and education. As Norlie asserted, "In times past much has been said of what America has done for the immigrant. America has done much for the immigrant. But there is also another side to this question. The immigrant has also done much for America."[28] The organizers presented this "inspiring history" in an effort to unite disparate members of the Norwegian-American community within a symbolic invocation of "peculiarity" that was compatible with American ideals. With rhetoric such as Norlie's, the organizers hoped to preserve their positions within an ethnic community without posing a threat to American culture. From daily correspondence between festival organizers and massive publicity campaigns to the Centennial's religious services, civic orations, and historical pageant, leaders articulated the Norwegian cultural heritage and its role in America's greatness. The organizers attempted to involve a widespread, often divergent, community in the construction of such a narrative, which was directed at both the community itself and the larger American culture.

Ticket sales were initially aimed specifically at Norwegians, whether they could attend the Centennial or not, "for this is their only opportunity and the only means by which they can contribute to this tremendous enterprise." According to Quamme, the financial director, the "objective in every community should be to sell every adult Norwegian a coupon book, and their work should not be considered finished until the local committee has, through some of its members, interviewed every Norwegian within their given territory." Quamme predicted that not only would this system underwrite the finances of the Centennial, it would also "make every Norwegian in the U.S. and Canada thoroughly acquainted with the object and purpose of the centennial and arouse his highest and personal interest in it." Quamme argued that the Centennial would "then become a national people's movement, the banding together of a great number of people to a dominant purpose. . . . The real success of the Centennial will be the national interest, support and participation by the millions of Norwegians on the American continent. Let us make it a great movement of the people themselves, in which they participate personally, even though in a small way. It must be a democratic people's movement on a large scale. . . ."[29] Following Quamme's suggestion, the national slogan became "One Season Ticket to Every Man, Woman, and Child of Norse Descent." Such rhetoric underpinned the organizers' jeremiad, the purpose of which was to educate and contain Norwegian Americans within a particular vision of their ethnicity in the hopes of maintaining a viable ethnic community. Such containment was part of a "movement" to invent a Norwegian-American ethnicity within some very narrow class definitions and interests.

As the Centennial drew closer, however, ticket sellers were encouraged to sell to non-Norwegians as well. In fact, such sales and publicity were crucial to the organizers' narrative, furthering their effort to defuse the larger culture's hostility to difference. In one of the committee's periodic bulletins to local representatives, the committee for the first time overtly outlined the "dual purpose" of the Centennial. Not only was it to revitalize a heroic Norwegian past to the present Norwegian population, but to demonstrate "the contribution our race has made to American history, ideals, art, music . . ." to "non-Norse" as well. "It is evident that unless large numbers of non-Norse people attend the celebration and view the wonderful exhibits, the event will fall short of attaining one of its two principle purposes."[30] In May 1925, Quamme wrote to county ticket sellers, "Through our program, we will give our people a chance for self-expression. The cultural side of our life will be emphasized and the American people in general will become better acquainted with us and our ideals."[31] Such a dual vision of the celebration was broadcast to the public-at-large that same month by Gustav B. Wollan, Norwegian American and publicity director for WCCO radio. He told his audience, "There is one thing I sincerely desire to emphasize, that I cannot too strongly stress, and that is this: while the coming Norwegian-American Centennial is being put on by the Norwegian Americans . . . it is by no means FOR them alone. It is for all of you. It is for ALL Americans to be interested in—for [we all helped in] developing American civilization and writing each its part of this truly romantic chapter of American history." Wollan informed his audience that this had been "the most interesting and important century in history, in which we Norwegian Americans have tried to impart the best of our national characteristics, ideals, depth of religious feeling, thrift—but, above all, our loyalty to the best country on earth."[32] This rhetorical strategy served both to claim power and status within American culture and to allay suspicions of disloyalty.

Such rhetoric, however, had to be negotiated among the organizers. In a letter from Kvale to Holstad, the congressman expressed his concern over whether the whole "Minnesota Delegation" in Congress would go together to invite the Secretary of State to the festivities, "irrespective of national origin, Norse, Irish, and whatnot." He asked Holstad, "Are we perhaps just a little too generous in inviting our brethren of other blood strain on this occasion? Please give me your candid opinion. I am not overly anxious to share with anyone who may not appreciate it the honor of belonging to the Viking race. On the other hand, we want to do everything possible to make our celebration a tremendous success."[33] The meaning of "success" went beyond the number of tickets sold, though this of course was an important consideration. In one of the weekly bulletins, Holstad quoted from a recent newspaper story chronicling the purchase of two tickets by Harvey Grimmer, "a staunch Irish Catholic," from T. P. Anderson, a "Norwegian Lutheran." The reporter wrote humorously of the "Norse-Irish Centennial" and headlined his story, "Peace Reigns!"[34] At the same time that they projected an image of themselves as good Americans, the organizers' effort at inclusivity was a statement that the immigrant story was the American story. It was a story that was safe and, indeed, harmonizing.

These rhetorical strategies were mirrored by a massive publicity campaign in both Norwegian-language and American newspapers around the country. Articles stressed the necessity for Norwegians to unite in a renewed confidence in their past and present accomplishments and for Americans to appreciate Norwegian contributions to their culture. A March *Minneapolis Journal* editorial asserted, "It is already manifest that the affair is to have the happy effect of bringing together in unwonted union the people of this widely gathered strain of blood. Differences of politics, religion, social distinction, business, whatnot—all are forgotten in the impulse for a reunion of Norsemen everywhere." And a *New York Times* article of February emphasized the contributions of Norwegian immigrants, who "have proved themselves to be hard-working, diligent people, earnest in their desire to become absorbed into American life, and at the same time contributing to it the fine qualities which they had brought with them from their seagirt homes."[35]

Such "unwonted union," however, was a narrative device that requires decoding before we can fully understand the organizers' vision of their world. As anthropologists have demonstrated, celebrations are "texts" that depict, interpret, and inform their social contexts. If it is in their interest, those who control the celebration ritualize their position "in order to sustain and legitimize it." As anthropologist Frank E. Manning has put it,

"Dynamic celebrations are symbolic (but important, and quite 'real') battlefields for waging competitive struggles for power, prestige and material objectives."[36] Part of this struggle is making choices about what and whom to include and to exclude. In his discussion of "the narrative construction of reality," Stuart Hall argues that, out of a complex web of myths and images, we construct narratives about history and events that "underpin," "reinforce," and "strengthen" particular understandings of the world. Such selective construction of reality "by definition undermine[s], weaken[s], and make[s] less powerful and important the alternative ways" of understanding the world. One way to begin to understand the "constructedness" of such a narrative, according to Hall, is to identify "the silences in a particular form . . . see where the absences and silences are, and you can begin to interrogate the seamless web of that particular story from the viewpoint of another story, as it were."[37] Raymond Williams has pointed out that all traditionalizing processes are selective and depend on both inclusions and exclusions.[38] Such selectivity tells us much about the meaning of any invented tradition or story. The Centennial organizers constructed a narrative of Norwegian-American history and ethnicity in the 1920s that attempted a compatibility with American history and culture, not only through the stories they did tell in their correspondence, publicity, and the celebration itself, but through the stories they chose not to tell. They told stories of Vikings and pioneers who helped to found modern civilization rather than stories about the many Norwegian men and women involved in attempts to radically transform American society through class and gender politics. Through both their inclusions and their exclusions, organizers created a story that masked the long history of debates and dissension among Norwegian Americans about politics and ethnicity.

After Coolidge praised Norwegian Americans for their contributions—read "assimilability"—Secretary of State Kellogg reiterated the president's main points, but ended with an explicit warning about radicalism. "Alien races do not always so easily assimilate. You have performed your duties of citizenship. I doubt if you are aware of the amount of destructive, revolutionary propaganda which is being secretly distributed in this country by foreign influence. If these people are not satisfied with our government and our institutions, let them go where they can find a government which does satisfy them. This is no place for them. . . ."[39] Of course, Kellogg, whose political career as a conservative, Republican, Scandinavian American was consistently challenged by left-leaning Norwegian-American politicians, was well aware of the radical heritage of Norwegians involved in farmer and labor politics, as we have seen. Embedded in many of the debates and discussions of ethnicity and Americanization in the community from the 1870s through World War I, was an argument about the efficacy of industrial capitalism. For many Norwegian Americans, this translated into radical political activity.

While there were certainly notable exceptions to this rule, particularly after World War I, a proportionately large number of Norwegians in this period practiced left-of-center politics. Jon Wefald has argued that the Norwegians were "unrelentingly progressive, frequently radical." According to Wefald, their politics were uniformly left-of-center, varying from progressivism and radical Republicanism to populism and socialism. In fact, the Norwegian Americans stood far enough to the left during the period from the 1890s to World War I to be ranked as one of the most consistently reform-bent ethnic groups in American history." While this may be a sweeping generalization, it is clear from Wefald's evidence of political activity and comment from the immigrant press that many Norwegians in this period did find themselves allied with third-party politics against mainstream American capitalist political parties. In the period from 1850–1880, Norwegians participated in local politics in great numbers and by 1880–1890 they entered state and national politics with a vengeance. The president of the Minnesota Viking League addressed this new phase by declaring that Norwegians and other Scandinavians "should deliver politically one tremendous blow . . . to teach the silk stocking, blue blood Yankees that the Scandinavians are not descendants of the lower conditions in nature." This statement indicates not only that the speaker is setting himself against "Yankee" capitalists, but also that the Scandinavians were objects of Anglo-American nativism. Here is evidence that ethnicity and politics were closely intertwined and that Norwegian Americans felt keenly the effects of American nativism. An 1895 Norwegian-language newspaper put it this way: "Let us move rapidly against bondage and tyranny and let us not hesitate to use politics." Between 1882 and 1924, Norwegians in the upper Midwest elected five senators, nineteen congressmen, eleven governors, eight lieutenant governors, eight secretaries of state, and four attorneys general. While not all were "uniformly left-of-center," by 1917 they were a powerful force in the more liberal wings of the Republican party and in growing third-party movements that focused on agrarian radicalism, including the Nonpartisan League.[40]

Wefald argues that these political activities rose most profoundly out of Norwegian folk culture. According to Wefald, whether La Follette Republicans in Wisconsin, radical Republicans in South Dakota, Nonpartisan

Leaguers in North Dakota, or Farmer-Laborites in Minnesota, the Norwegian members of these political groups shared a common cultural heritage that emphasized a cooperative commonwealth over predatory capitalism. And when conditions were right, Norwegians brought this world view to bear on their politics. Certainly the above quotation demonstrates at least the perception that "Norwegian" and "capitalist" were antithetical terms. While this may tell part of the story, additional influences must be stressed. First, specific agricultural and economic conditions in this period encouraged radical movements, though they may have called up memories of agrarian unrest in Norway which many immigrants in this period had indeed experienced.[41] And second, progressive politics and third-party movements were a national phenomenon because of those very economic conditions. Midwestern politics must be viewed in this context. Furthermore, among Norwegian Americans, class and regional identities may have been equally—or more—powerful motivators for getting involved in radical politics. However, in terms of Norwegian identification, it is important to note that these politics were spoken of in ethnic terms among Norwegian Americans themselves. It became an important badge of ethnicity in fiction if not in fact. While the numbers of Norwegians actually involved in radical politics has been debated, this link between radical politics and ethnicity had practical ramifications for Norwegians in the context of the heightened nativist movement during World War I and the Red Scare that followed. And it was a link that was suppressed by the Centennial organizers.

Knute Nelson was the most notable example of Norwegian-American politicians who took a conservative Republican stance. In the elections of 1920, for example, there were deep divisions between Republicans like Nelson and Nonpartisan League–endorsed candidates like Henrik Shipstead, O. J. Kvale, and Knud Wefald. In an editorial in the Norwegian-language press, Nelson criticized the radical members of his community. "The bitterness and malignity of the Norwegian nonpartisan farmers exceeds that of any other class of Nonpartisans. . . . It is only the older class of Norwegian immigrants and their descendants that seem [to] stand fast in the Republican faith—the rest seem to be in a state of flux and chaos. . . ." Despite Nelson's comments, there were two important appeals to La Follette, the Nonpartisan League, and Farmer-Labor progressivism in the immediate postwar period. The first appeal countered the big business politics of Presidents Harding and Coolidge, which was perceived to be antifarmer. And the second countered foreign policies that could lead to another loyalist crusade.[42]

However, by 1925 the Farmer-Labor party, which had risen to the forefront after the Nonpartisan League dissolved, took a more moderate stand in terms of social transformation. Former Nonpartisan Leaguers Shipstead, Kvale, and Wefald were now politicians who "called for a redress of grievances within the existing system, not a radical restructuring of the system."[43] These three congressmen were intimately involved in the planning and organization of the Centennial. The narrative that they helped to construct masked the political divisions that still existed in their community and denied the radical heritage that continued to be so important to many Norwegian Americans. In an early version of the Centennial program, Andrew Furuseth, president of the Seamen's Union, was scheduled to speak on "The Contribution of the Norwegian Element to the Organized Labor Movement in America." In April 1925, however, Shipstead alerted the Centennial committee that he had been unable to reach Furuseth about speaking on the program. He wrote, "I have been unable to get anyone to write an essay on 'Norsemen in the Labor Movement.' This I regret. I hope you can get someone to do it."[44] While this letter appears to indicate otherwise, there were many Norwegian Americans—at all levels of activity—involved in labor politics and organizations in the 1920s, including two of six committee members who originated the plans for the revolutionary Franklin Co-Operative Creamery after the 1919–1920 milk drivers' strikes.[45] In the May 1925 edition of the creamery's newsletter, the editor publicized the Centennial celebration, noting that "a large number of [the creamery's] officers and employees are descendants of these hardy Norse pioneers. . . ."[46] Indeed, eleven of sixteen founders and directors of the creamery were of Scandinavian descent.[47] The "inability" to find someone to speak about Norwegian Americans in the labor movement served the ideological purposes of the organizers. In their reconstruction of Norwegian-American history, labor's part in Norwegian contributions to radical politics was less important than their contribution as Norwegians to the building of American democracy.

Politics based on gender were nearly as absent as labor politics from the Centennial celebration—a more startling fact given that the head of the women's committee, Caroline Storlie, was an active member of the National Woman's party, the radical voice in the women's movement. Storlie supervised the female chairs of each state, the majority of whom were professionals and / or active in voluntary ethnic associations or reform movements. In addition to their work promoting the celebration and collecting memorabilia and heirlooms, women were assigned to the following areas and tasks during the celebration: the nursery, the hospital, lost and found, the rest rooms, assisting at souvenir booths, meeting the trains of out-of-town guests, and looking out for "the welfare and comfort of those attending the Centennial."[48] While such activity was in keeping to some extent with the politicized domesticity of a large segment of the women's movement, there is evidence that this was not unproblematic. For example, in a circular letter to twenty-eight Wisconsin counties, Mrs. G. H. Niland opened her request for county chairs with the following: "For some inscrutable reason the Women's Auxiliary Committee has assigned to me the task of organizing the Norwegian women of Wisconsin to an active part in promoting the success of the impending celebration of the Norwegian-American Centennial. No doubt, too, it has been thought that along certain lines women are better adapted to accomplish the things sought for. This might be especially true along the line of ferreting out relics, curios. . . ."[49]

The irony evident in this statement points to the problematic domesticated nature of the work assigned to women. Mary Wee noted to Storlie that she "could tell some very interesting stories about the days when men were averse and afraid to let us do anything outside the home—and some of the women were no better."[50] Nevertheless, Storlie attempted to create a women's program that was politically charged by inviting as speakers prominent Norwegian women involved in politics in their home country and Thorstein Veblen, known for his virulent critiques of American culture. Veblen declined and one community member lamented to Storlie that "our most original and productive thinker" could not attend.[51] And while some of the Norwegian women were present, the women's program was filled with relatively innocuous speeches that reflected the larger narrative of the organizers. Hannah Astrup Larsen, editor of *The American-Scandinavian Review* and descendant of the first Norwegian woman to emigrate and settle in America, delivered the opening speech. Larsen honored the strong pioneer women who helped to settle the continent, whose particular contribution had its roots in a Norwegian tradition of respect between men and women. "As far back as 'Ejaal's Saga' we read of Bergthora's saying, 'I am Ejaal's wife and I have as much to say in our household as he has.' " Larsen told her audience that while Norwegian-American men held to these traditions in the home, they were slower to translate it into respect and equality outside the home. However, she asserted, there had been a "veritable revolution in the position of Norwegian-American women. . . . As teachers and writers, and in executive positions women have ample opportunities for stamping the image of their ideals on our community."[52] At the same time that this speech addressed issues of gender politics,

Larsen displaced them onto the past. In the context of a continuing battle for women's rights, in which many Norwegian-American women were involved, Larsen told her audience that the war had been won.

Perhaps the most persuasive evidence that the women involved in the celebration were disappointed with their representation is the fact that *after* the celebration, they organized into the Norse-American Centennial Daughters and published a collection of essays, including Larsen's, titled *Norse-American Women, 1825–1925*. Indeed, according to the group's president, Josephine Brack, the group's first action was to endorse Alma Gutterson's idea that the record of the Centennial be preserved. As Brack put it in 1945, "the men were cold on endorsing her proposition, but I am very proud to state that on July 13, 1925, after 87 women had decided to reorganize . . . the *first action* taken" was to endorse the book. Highlighting the importance of this endeavor in terms of their roles as women, Brack commented, "The woman's committee performed a real job—in fact such a good big job that they often clashed in committee and more often with the *big shots*. But we all know our Norwegian men. They can't get along without us but they like to steal the show (Brack's emphasis)."[53]

The essays in the Centennial Daughters' book vacillated between the two strands of the women's movement—first, politicized domesticity and the republican mother, and second, the commitment to eliminating all forms of difference between men and women, namely, subjection. In both cases, the women harkened back to Norway for the roots of these beliefs. Indeed, the Minnesota branch of the National Woman's Party in Washington, D.C., sent a letter of appreciation to the Women's Auxiliary, thanking them for inviting women of Norway, who had done so much "for the advancement of woman and her equality before the law."[54] While this effort paralleled the rhetorical strategy of the organizers' narrative, its taint of political radicalism made it unsuitable for the celebration itself. For while the women's movement in each of these manifestations was by and large a middle-class movement, in the 1920s it operated within an increasingly hostile environment. The bureaucratic state and the consumer culture continued to undercut efforts at civic and communal organization. And the traditional notion of women as moral guardians within the home fit well into the increasingly entrenched corporate economy.[55] Collecting relics and heirlooms connected to home life and family were "safer" occupations for the women involved in the Centennial than an assertion of an ethnic heritage that legitimated political activity.

Just as the Centennial organizers distanced themselves from the political activity of laborers and women, they forged explicit alliances with the

Fig. 9: President Coolidge and his entourage drive down the parade route to cheering crowds in Minneapolis. *Courtesy Minnesota Historical Society.*

business community. In early 1925, campaign organizer Clarence Winter offered his company's services to the committee. "It is our firm belief," he wrote, "that the Centennial is deserving of the support of the business interests of Saint Paul and Minneapolis to an extent sufficient to cover the cost of staging the celebration."[56] Indeed, in addition to advances from the state legislature and Norwegian-American associations, the Centennial committee received money from both cities' civic and commerce associations, banks, and corporations. Twin Cities' manufacturers decided to reschedule their Northwest Industrial Exposition to coincide with the Centennial, noting that it would "be a wonderful opportunity to show these two hundred thousand or more visitors what we manufacture in the Northwest."[57] The explicit connection to area businesses is particularly evident in a letter from publicity director Oscar Arneson, in which he argues that the preparations for the Centennial were not moving forward with "sufficient momentum." He had arrived at this impression from his conversations with "civic associations" and "business men's associations." He urged the publicity committee to "put a little extra pep into the proceedings from this time on. . . ."[58] Business interests clearly had a stake in the Centennial's success.

In addition, the Twin Cities decorated their streets and buildings in conjunction with the Centennial celebration in general, and the parade for President Coolidge in particular. The St. Paul Association and the Minneapolis Civic and Commerce Association proposed the parade and took charge of the details with the cooperation of the Centennial directors. The assistant secretary of the MCCA noted to Holstad that "the hospitality and friendliness of the Minneapolis people can be [best] obtained by decorative effects. It is for that reason that we are so gladly co-operating with other business organizations in making arrangements for an extensive display of the Norse Centennial."[59]

Of course, in addition to demonstrating the city's "hospitality and friendliness," the "extensive display" of Norwegian and American flags and banners promoted the city's businesses. Dayton's Department Store, for example, photographed two versions of its extensively decorated storefront. One is touched up to resemble a painting. The Dayton's building is abstracted from its surroundings and draped with Norwegian and American flags down its height with smaller banners depicting both a Viking ship and the immigrant ship alternating above the first level. The second photograph depicts President Coolidge—"the business of this country is business" president—waving from an automobile in front of the Dayton's building. Both photographs appear to have been used by Dayton's for advertising purposes. The success of such efforts by the organizers was evident in the souvenir program, which boasted a series of advertisements by local businesses, each praising the Norwegians for their good citizenship. In addition, the local papers carried advertisements that used the Centennial and the prospect of thousands of visitors to the city to sell their products. The Public Drug Company, for example, bought a full-page ad for a "Norse-American Centennial Drug Sale." Donaldson's Department Store in its ad welcomed visitors in Norwegian, advertising "Special Norwegian Dishes" in the cafeteria, Norwegian music in the tea room, and Norwegian-speaking guides dressed in national costume.[60]

The exclusion of radical politics combined with the inclusion of business interests connoted a clear class position. The image of Norwegian-American ethnicity promoted by the organizers was decidedly middle class and upwardly mobile. The class differences that existed within the community were nowhere more eloquently stated than in a letter from D. H. Bahlrud, a Norwegian-Canadian from Edmonton, to the Centennial committee. Because he had founded the Sons of Norway in that community, the committee asked him to organize Edmonton for the celebration. Bahlrud, however, informed the committee that it would be impossible for "anybody to interest the people here in the Centennial or anything else that is worthy of a Norwegian." According to Bahlrud, a manual laborer, he and his family were "shunned" by every notable Norwegian in Edmonton.[61] Such bitterness spoke to the tremendous class differences within the community, differences that the committee attempted to mask in their construction of Norwegian-American history.

This middle-class conception was particularly evident in debates over the Centennial's exhibits. One such exhibit was a display of art by Norwegian painters and sculptors, most of which was loaned by Norwegian-American owners. Tollef Quam, a local community member, wrote to organizer Herborg Reque, protesting the use of Norwegian artists over Norwegian-American artists. "We shouldn't pride ourselves with loaned feathers," he scolded.[62] In her answer, Reque corrected Quam, noting that most of the artwork to be exhibited was indeed created by Norwegian Americans. As for the exhibit of Norwegian art, she argued, "our intention . . . is to emphasize the fact that many of our pioneers came from homes of culture in Norway, that they brought works of art with them and had a background of art which affected their development here. This because the American public in general think all the Norwegian pioneers to this country were peasants that brought nothing with them."[63] By invoking such standards of taste and prestige, the organizers aimed their message at an American audience whose acceptance they desired. Knut Gjerset's organization of the historical exhibits provides further evidence of this class effort. For example, the displays of Norwegian homes of 1825 were of both the peasant- and merchant-class. These, in combination with the "refined," contemporary Norwegian home, would demonstrate, according to Gjerset, that "the homes in Norway are not crude and primitive as is generally believed by people here." He was also concerned about proposed displays of national peasant costumes and other activities of peasant life and culture. Such features, he wrote to Bothne, "may have a dramatic effect, but the American people will get the idea that we are a crude and primitive people without real culture."[64] The representation of "real culture," according to the organizers' conceptions, was clearly class-based and aimed at assuaging the doubts of a mainstream culture that seriously questioned any display of ethnic identity.

The heavy emphasis on the Twin Cities and business interests was not without its opponents. The most consistent criticism came out of Luther College in Decorah, Iowa, the site of the Norwegian pioneer museum. There has been a long-standing competition between Luther College, which catered to the rural working class, and St. Olaf College, which drew more largely from the Twin Cities. This rivalry was evident in the 1920s in competing conceptions of Norwegian-American ethnicity. In November 1925, Oscar Olson forwarded to Holstad a copy of a speech he gave at the meeting of Luther College's Centennial Committee. He argued that the tentative program for the celebration, with its speeches by "outsiders," (i.e., President Coolidge), and sessions run by Twin Cities organizations, was not reflective of all Norwegian Americans. Olson wanted more local Norwegians to give speeches about Norwegian-American accomplishments in farming, pioneer life, literature, art, and other areas. He asserted that a permanent program should be prepared to "enlist the best efforts of some of the Norwegians who labored in the heat of the day and far into the night."[65] A month later, O. M. Norlie, a Luther College professor, reiterated Olson's suggestions in a detailed, four-page letter to the committee, noting again that the celebration should represent all Norwegian Americans. "I'm sure that our people will never be satisfied if all the committees and speakers are to be made up of men from Minneapolis and St. Paul. Even though people generally admit that all the brightest lights finally turn up in the Twin Cities."[66] The obvious bitterness and competition notwithstanding, the committee incorporated Olson's and Norlie's suggestions into their plans and organizations, resulting in a program that combined contemporary interests with an extensive exhibit of Norwegian-American history and contributions to nearly every aspect of American life. Indeed, the two were not incompatible, but worked in tandem to present a narrative of Norwegian-American history that paralleled Anglo-American progressive history.

Underpinning this narrative were the two migrations of Norwegians to the New World—the Vikings and the pioneers. The Viking story, based on the old sagas passed along through centuries of Norwegian folklore, provided images of courage, triumph, and early democratic ideals. And, of course, there was the claim to discovery: according to the legend, Leif Ericson, a Norwegian, was the first European to set foot on what would become the North American continent. The saga of the nineteenth-century migration was equally important. Not only did these pioneer farmers contribute materially to building the Northwest, as did pioneers of all national origins, but they brought with them the democratic and religious ideals that had been cultivated in Norway since the pagan Viking era. This rhetorical strategy, rooted in these two stories, became the basis upon which the organizers constructed their narrative.

Two of the main souvenirs created for the Centennial provide powerful visual evidence of this strategy. To mark the occasion, Norwegian Americans in Congress convinced the government to produce both a commemorative medal and two commemorative stamps. The medal was struck instead of a coin because of the attitude in Congress resulting generally from the prevailing anti-hyphenism and specifically from an "agitation" in 1924 over a Huguenot-Walloon Tercentenary half dollar. Members of Congress criticized the coin as a vehicle for religious propaganda and as therefore "un-American" and "unsuitable" for U.S. coinage.[67] Congressman Kvale, the chief actor in this drama, negotiated carefully to avoid any taint of anti-Americanism. In his speech inviting Congress to attend the Centennial, he assured them, "I am well aware that to some of you gentlemen the prefix 'Norse', or any prefix, may seem to indicate something not purely and truly American. If the prefix in this case implied anything even faintly suggesting such a possibility, I would be the first to repudiate it in the most emphatic and unqualified terms."[68] The approval of the U.S. Congress was crucial to the organizers' narrative. In a press release about both the medal and the stamps, the committee noted that "never before in the history of the U.S. has the celebration of an historic event been so uniquely and signally honored by the American government as has the Norwegian-American Centennial." The inscription on the medal, "Authorized by the Congress of the United States," was particularly striking, according to the

Fig. 10: Two sides of the souvenir medal struck with the permission of the U.S. Congress. Both sides signify Viking exploration. *Courtesy Norwegian-American Historical Society.*

committee: "The true significance of this is so apparent as to need no comment."[69]

The medal that was approved by Congress does not depict Norwegian arrival to an already formed American culture; rather, the design is of a full-length Viking chieftain who has left his ship and come ashore on the American continent. The dates 1825 and 1925 flank either side of the figure. A Viking ship and the date A.D. 1000, the year of Leif Ericson's purported discovery of America, is inscribed on the reverse. While one of the stamps

Fig. 11: Two souvenir stamps issued by the U.S. Post Office. The stamp on the left depicts a Viking ship, while the one on the right represents the immigrant sloop. *Courtesy Norwegian-American Historical Society.*

depicts the immigrant ship in sail, the other is a design of a Viking ship. Some organizers expressed concern that the Viking chieftain be linked so specifically to the date "1825," noting that the two migrations were of quite different people. The visual imagery, however, supports the organizers' narrative and the significant links that were made between the two migrations.

As Lovoll has recently pointed out, a powerful "ethnic mythology" existed around the figure of Leif Ericson at least from the 1874 publication of Rasmus B. Anderson's *America Not Discovered by Columbus.*[70] In 1901, for example, the Norwegian-American community in Chicago built a statue of Ericson in Humboldt Park. In the 1920s, Norwegian-Americans celebrated Ericson with a "renewed vigor." In honor of Oslo's Bishop Johan Lunde, visiting Brooklyn en route to the Centennial celebration, that city named an area in Brooklyn "Leif Ericson Square" with the promise of a future statue. A group from Philadelphia called "Leif's Order" reserved a room on the Centennial fairgrounds to show slides and promote a national Leif Ericson celebration. The Ericson myth was important to the Norwegian-American reconstruction of history because his discovery was evidence of prior claim. More crucial, however, was the general history of Viking exploration. In a letter to the Brooklyn Board of Aldermen regarding "Leif Ericson Square," the mayor of New York waxed eloquently about the significance of this mythology: "The City of New York is determined . . . to embalm in our records, for present and future generations, an adequate recognition of the bold men of the North whose spirit of conquest and adventure spurred on the later periods of discovery and exploration which made out of an unknown region the greatest nation under the canopy of God's blue heaven."[71] Hence, the Viking chieftain on the medal was Ericson as a romanticized ideal. In the Centennial narrative, such a heritage evoked not only courage and independence but also a worldwide, centuries-long influence of Nordic culture. As the mayor's statement demonstrates, the myth advanced the Norwegian-Americans' claim to status and power at the same time that it invoked typically "American" values of discovery and linear history.

Typical of this construction of history was Frederick Stevenson's article of May 24, 1925, in the *Brooklyn Daily Beagle*. Referring to the Ericson discovery, Stevenson argues that the Norwegians actually "made the United States possible. They were the first to break ground here and declare their independence. . . . Other races came here when the land was plowed and the streets were paved in the cities. America is America today because of the Nordics. Let us join in the celebration. Honors are Even!" Stevenson argued that only the Romans and the ancient Nordics, who "had never submitted to the Roman yoke," had left lasting impressions of their laws, government, society, and "positive character" on the "civilized communities of the world today." Indeed, he continued, English rulers were descendants of the Norwegians, and despite the fact that the English continue to insist on the Anglo-Saxon "backbone of England," it was really the "influence of these Norse conquerors that gave England her place in world history." Such rhetoric was a crucial component of the organizers' narrative from the earliest planning stages. In 1923 Oscar Arneson, who would become publicity chairman, outlined the importance of the Viking heritage. According to Arneson, the first Viking migration of "war-lords, earls, and petty rulers" began as a protest to a totalitarian ruler.[72] In the Norwegian construction of history, this independent spirit became deeply rooted in Norwegian culture, out of which grew the well-known traits of egalitarianism and democracy. One Norwegian American reflected this conception of history when he suggested to the planning committee that "the keynote of the pageant should be that men of Norse blood have those qualities that make for desirable American citizenship and that the earlier Norse immigrants not only conformed to American standards and ideals but were among the very people who created them."[73]

As Professor Norlie pointed out in the program, the original American settlers had already been greatly influenced by "Norse blood," both figuratively and literally. Therefore, it was not necessary for Norwegians to assimilate into American culture, for they possessed even more deeply than New Englanders so-called American ideals. This idea was prevalent throughout the Centennial, even in the daily correspondence of committee members. For example, in a response to Lieutenant Colonel Hume in the Office of the Surgeon General about a government presentation to visiting Norwegian dignitaries, Bothne ends on the following note: "It was indeed a pleasure to me to learn of your personal interest in our celebration and the fact that you have Norse blood in your veins." Bothne assumed this fact because "Hume" is a Scottish name. And "in Scotland, England, and Ireland, there are many traces of Norse influences and in a review of the Norse achievements in history, such as the contemplated celebration should be, this ought not to be forgotten."[74] By invoking adventure, exploration, conquest and independence, the organizers appealed equally to a Norwegian identity and to American patriotism. The cultural values attributed to the Viking age by these Norwegian Americans were deemed perfectly compatible to American values in the "symbolic umbrella" constructed by the Centennial organizers.

The significance placed on this conception of Viking history was also the foundation for the organizers' construction of pioneer history. In his May article, Stevenson argued that the descendants of these conquerors who settled in the Midwest beginning in 1825 have "made up that sturdy and industrious population of farmers and producers which is keeping America on her legs. . . ."[75] An explicit connection between these two migrations was made by Wollan in an advertisement dedicated to the Centennial by Schuneman and Evans clothiers in St. Paul. "The Saga of Wheatland" recounted the migratory nature of the "Norsemen." Wollan wrote, "Warlike they were a thousand years ago, messengers of peace today, yet the victories of peace should have no less a place in the Sun than the blood-bought paeans of Victory of olden days." Wollan reiterated the claims made by other organizers about the Norwegian roots of Anglo-European and American democracy. Even in those Norwegians who did not follow these early adventurers, according to Wollan, "the Viking spirit lived on and on, deeply and firmly rooted in the hardy Norse character." This spirit "awoke" after nearly a thousand years and "a sturdy little band of 52 men, women, and children" set sail for America. The latter-day Vikings "blazed the trail" and settled the west. "Today," Wollan ended his saga, "a scant hundred years since the beginning of the Norsemen's second migration to America, the little band of 52 has grown to 2,500,000 of Viking blood on American soil. Toil, hardship, sacrifice, struggle with the primeval marked the beginnings. Ease, comfort, happiness succeeded as the numbers grew. THEY BECAME AMERICANS ALL. Of such is 'The Saga of Wheatland.' "[76] Caroline Storlie also made such a connection between the two migrations in a 1924 letter to local organizers, urging them to form Centennial committees. She argued that the American frontier appealed to the wandering spirit and adventurous imagination of the Norwegians, who were "endowed with a sacred heritage, a love of liberty, a spirit of personal worth, and faith in God." With such a heritage, they enriched "American thought as they had enriched old Europe centuries ago."[77] In yet another advertisement, Dayton's Department Store published a print depicting a Viking ship suspended in the clouds over a farmer pushing a plow through rich farmland. Dayton's offered souvenir copies to anyone who requested them. In an accompanying text, Dayton's thanked Norwegian Americans, "who have played a leading part in the development of the Northwest. To the peaceful and helpful pursuits of agriculture and business they have brought their vigor and aggressiveness, the industry and zeal, with which their ancestors conquered the rocky shores of Norway and the uncharted western seas."[78]

The Norwegians' use of the pioneer symbol in the 1920s was not unique. As Bodnar points out in his work on commemorative events, the pioneer symbol was popular in the late nineteenth and early twentieth centuries, for "its appeal to ordinary people resided in its vernacular meaning of sturdy ancestors who founded ethnic communities and families, preserved traditions in the face of social change and overcame hardship." These pioneer symbols, according to Bodnar, expressed anxieties about increasing industrialization and economic centralization. Indeed, officials "attempted to redefine" the pioneer as more symbolic of the building of a nation, industrialization and all.[79] The pioneer symbol worked well for the organizers of the Centennial, for they combined both a vernacular and official meaning. They epitomized the sturdy ancestors who carried on worthy traditions, but who nevertheless contributed to developing the Northwest, both agriculturally and industrially.

The pioneer "saga" told by the organizers was continuous with the Viking heritage with two important distinctions. The emigrants of 1825 were not "war lords" and "earls," but poor farmers and Quakers, escaping sweeping economic changes and religious persecution. This fact only enhanced the narrative's emphasis on courage and spirit. Secondly, these migrants were not pagan, but Christian, and organizers emphasized the powerful role of religion as a particularly potent contribution of modern Norwegian Americans to American culture. In a speech given at the Centennial, Oscar Olson, president of Luther College, commented on the fact that the Norwegian cultural heritage made Norwegians good Americans, connecting both the pagan and Christian aspects of that heritage: "It has made us good American citizens; and, as the offspring of a free and enlightened people, who trace their racial descent from the Vikings and their spiritual descent from Martin Luther and the great Reformation, has enabled us to contribute worthily to American progress."[80] In an article in the *Minneapolis Daily Star,* the writer makes an explicit connection between secular and spiritual pursuits. He points out that "Norse" farmers are thrifty and industrious, virtues "held in high esteem by the Norwegian Lutheran Church."[81] Organizers asserted that, from the original sloopers to their present-day descendants, "the faith of the fathers has been the most dominating and characteristic influence among them." Thus, they pointed out, "it is most fitting that the Norse-American Centennial should devote the opening day of the celebration proper to praise and thanksgiving to the Giver of all good things, who has so marvelously prospered them and theirs in the New World."[82] In a "Norse-American Centennial Cantata," published by the Centennial Committee of the Norwegian Lu-

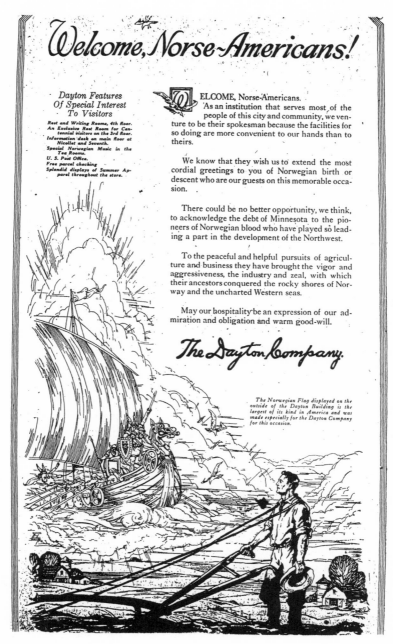

Fig. 12: Dayton's Department Store advertisement, *Minneapolis Journal*, 6 June, 1925, in honor of the celebration.

Fig. 13: Church and state dignitaries gather during the Centennial in front of Secretary of State Kellogg's home. *Courtesy Minnesota Historical Society.*

theran Church, composer B. J. Rothnem wrote, "America gave, but she also received a culture through ages of progress achieved. And this be her greatness, her gift and renown: A people's devotion to God! This be our Crown!"[83]

That one day of the festival was devoted almost entirely to worship is testament to the organizers' belief in a powerful religious heritage among the Norwegians and their need to reinforce that belief within the larger festival narrative. In a Centennial program article concerning the contributions of the Norwegians, the author writes, "The contributions made by the Norse element of our population to the spiritual and cultural life of America are of greatest importance and show a rare spirit of sacrifice and devotion. The Norwegian pioneers were a serious-minded people of strong religious convictions. . . ."[84] Paradoxically, though religion played an important role in the festivities, the NLCA was only tangentially involved in organizing the Centennial. Early in the organizing, the committee invited all Norwegian organizations and church bodies to aid in the planning, and the NLCA church council took charge of inviting religious dignitaries. Not until April 7, 1925, did the directors appeal to pastors "for their support of the Centennial by urging their people to attend and to purchase tickets in advance." And on May 13, directors passed a resolution which was sent to pastors concerning the "divine festal service" which would open the Centennial. The program committee made arrangements for four services, "two . . . to be conducted in the Norwegian language and two in the English language, so all our people may have the opportunity to take part in these services of prayer, praise, and thanksgiving. . . ." The resolution further stated that the directors realized "that the attendance at these services will to a certain extent be the standard by which our religious life will be measured"; therefore, they requested that all clergy urge their members to attend one of these services.[85]

Though there is no direct evidence for this, the relative marginality of the church from the main organizational structures may have been an attempt by the organizers to distance the event from the debates over language and other matters of integration and identity that were still plaguing the church. Instead, they desired an abstract sense of religion and spirituality that would prove them worthy Americans. In his discussion of the immigrant church in America, Bodnar points to the usefulness of Timothy Smith's argument about "the pervasive attachment between ethnic identification and religion in immigrant America as a process by which ethnic groups mobilized to pursue political and economic agendas."[86] As Bodnar points out, there were frequent disagreements, of course, over what ends to pursue and how to pursue them, as the organizers' tenuous link to the religious establishment suggests.

The religious services, conducted in both Norwegian and English, were attended by crowds "exceeding the average State Fair day." As one journalist reported in the June 8, 1925, edition of the *Minneapolis Journal,* "Despite a beating sun that drove the mercury upward and turned the entire Fair grounds into a sweltering arena . . . every seat, every box was filled. . . . scores stood in the aisles so no one could move. At every entrance, others stood, all through the two hour service." At the service, Bishop Lunde, visiting from Norway, read several telegrams from Norwegian congregations who were conducting services that day with the Centennial in mind. But Dr. H. G. Stub, seventy-six-year-old head of the NLCA, "sounded the keynote of the day."

> Our love remains strong for that land where life was an endless fight against a strong soil and a stormy sea. A land poor in gold, but where almost every child can read or write. But stronger than these ties are the bonds of faith and hope and Christian charity—that Christianity given us by our people. Norsemen came to America 50 or 100 years ago hoping for an easier and a better living, but found the heaviest kind of work. They fought Indians and grasshoppers, they answered the call of President Lincoln for men. And now this people is holding its place in its adopted country with honor. Our prayers go upward that all that is done may be for the good of our country, America.

The journalist quoting this speech concluded with this observation: "Like the murmur of the sea came the sound of thousands of voices a minute later repeating in Norwegian the words of the Lord's prayer. . . ."[87] These religious services added a sacred dimension to the Centennial's larger historical narrative. The purported religious heritage of the Norwegian people was intimately connected to the sacrifices they made as pioneers and as contributors to American society. Furthermore, an insistence on religious devotion set them apart for the larger culture's conception of "foreign radicalism" and reasserted the powerful role of the church and tradition in leadership in an increasingly fragmented community in the 1920s.

Both the Viking and pioneer heritages, as well as the connections made to Christianity, contributed to the progressive vision of the festival narrative. Arneson had argued in 1923 that "by remembering the noble work done by our fathers, we shall be inspired with greater zeal to prove ourselves worthy of being their children by clean living, by useful work for our community and our country. . . ."[88] Arneson's jeremiad became central to the organizers' conception of the celebration. An April 1925 press release stated, "It will be a great and grand review of 100 years of American history as exemplified in American citizenship of Norse ancestry. It will be educational, inspirational, and entertaining in the highest degree. . . . Those now living will . . . revive old memories, live again in the past, witness the pageant of 100 years of progress, and come home better Norsemen and better Americans."[89] At the celebration, the numerous orations given by civic, political, and intellectual leaders echoed this progressive imagery. Both the Norwegian- and English-language sessions were given over to discussions of the Norwegian cultural heritage and its role in American progress. Essays in the souvenir program chronicled Norwegian achievements in art, music, religion, politics, literature, science, and so on. Reflecting this progressive strategy, Wollan recounted in a press release the early Norse settlement of Muskego, Wisconsin, where the first steam sawmill in the New World was "built by a Norseman"; where the first Norsemen elected to state offices were born; and where were built "the first homes of many Norse immigrants and their descendants who later made names for themselves in various fields," including religion, journalism, medicine, and linguistics.[90] In another press release, the author recounted the first Norse settlement in Minnesota in 1850. "From this modest beginning," the Norwegians grew to 22 percent of the state's population and distinguished themselves in every profession. The press release ends with this typically Minnesotan understatement: "Not a bad accumulation for only 75 years!"[91]

Organized by Gjerset and with contributions from Norwegian Americans from all over the country, the Norse-American Exhibition program created a historical narrative that further reinforced the progressive thematic structure of the celebration. Accompanied by historical texts, the exhibit moved from models of Viking ships and antiquities from that period, through exhibits of pioneer life, through the role of churches and schools in immigrant culture, to agriculture, the immigrant press, literature, politics, and art. The exhibit then recounted the roles of charity and mutual aid societies, ethnic organizations, and women in maintaining cultural traditions. The exhibition ended with displays of Norwegian contributions to modern American life in terms of engineering, architecture, trade and commerce, industry, and war. A journalist for the *Minnesota Journal* described the exhibition with an emphasis on progress: "Past the relics of early days, the things that made homes for the early Norwegian pioneers, pushed all day long a never-ending stream of the pioneers' descendants. . . . In one little exhibit is typified the whole display. On one stand is a model of 'Per Viking's Farm, 1886'—three log cabins, a few cows, a wooden fence; on another, a model of 'Ole Viking's Farm, 1925'—an automobile in the driveway, electric lights and telephone in the house, modern immaculate barns, blooded stock. That is the keynote of it all."[92] Like the commemorative medal and stamps, the speeches and essays, and the extensive publicity releases, the exhibition promoted a progressive historical narrative within the context of a Norwegian cultural heritage that was compatible with American values of progress and consumption.

According to the July 1910, issue of *Century*, "Nothing is more likely to cement the sympathies of our people and to accentuate our homogeneity than a cultivation of pageants."[93] The *Pageant of the Northmen*, the culminating event of the celebration, combined all of the narrative elements of the celebration into a massive historical display. Like the organizers of the Anglo-American, progressive pageants referred to in *Century*, the Norwegian-American organizers presented a conflict-free, "homogenous" vision of Norwegian-American ethnicity that reinforced their larger, "nonthreatening" narrative. "Ritual dramas," as anthropologists have demonstrated, are an important element of celebrations. As Allesandro Falassi points out, the subject matter of these dramas "is often a creation myth, a foundation or migratory legend, or a military success particularly relevant in the mythical or historical memory of the community staging the festival." Through such dramas, the community is "reminded of a Golden Age, the trials and tribulations of their founding fathers in reaching the present location of the community. . . ." The "sacred story" is not always staged, but is "hinted at and referred to" in other parts of the celebration.[94] In the Centennial, organizers did both. As we have seen, the "sacred story" of the Vikings and pioneers, both a founding and a migratory legend, permeated the celebration. The pageant combined all of this discourse into a massive spectacle.

The intentionality (the design or form) and the enactment (the performance) of the pageant were both essential to its meaning.[95] Centennial organizers used a particularly American form—the historical pageant—to disseminate their "sacred story," and they presented this form in the context of their larger celebration. The images in the pageant were not accompanied by a verbal "text"; there was neither dialogue nor a narrator. Roland Barthes's ideas about communication are useful here in understanding how meaning was conveyed through the pageant. According to Barthes, verbal language serves to "anchor" the meaning of images. "The anchorage may be ideological and indeed this is its principle function; the text directs the reader through the signifieds of the image, causing him to avoid some and receive others; by means of an often subtle *dispatching* it remote-controls him toward a meaning chosen in advance."[96] But what of images without verbal language as the immediate "dispatcher"? What "anchored" the pageant imagery was the "text" preceding the performance in the rest of the celebration—the publicity, the speeches, the exhibits—and a shared knowledge of the pageant form. Such "anchoring" bolstered the organizers' larger narrative. Utilizing a familiar, progressive form, the organizers created a historical narrative that supported their representation of themselves as "safe" ethnics.

In his comprehensive study of American historical pageantry, David Glassberg argues that the pageant form was perhaps the most popular means of celebration for civic anniversaries during the Progressive Era. Before World War I, according to Glassberg, "historical pageantry flourished at the intersection of progressivism and antimodernism," placing "nostalgic imagery in a dynamic, future-oriented reform context." In America pageantry grew out of the civic celebrations of the late nineteenth century, which centered around historical orations in which speakers constructed "narratives of local community development alongside the religious rhetoric of nationalism to forge a united community of believers out of residents with diverse ethnic, class, and regional backgrounds." The earliest pageants were the result of a combined need to control the commercial spectacle elements that were creeping into civic celebrations, to disseminate "art and culture" to the American public, and, at the same time, to present a "picturesque Anglo-American past" that would teach the same lessons as the historical oration. Reformers and those whom Glassberg calls "genteel intellectuals" adopted and transformed elements of the Elizabethan revival in England to serve these purposes. Full of antimodern imagery, these pageants were attractive to both genteel intellectuals and members of patriotic societies because they "promised to elicit popular interest without sacrificing artistic standards and the marrow of Anglo-American history so important for the transmission of proper values and ideals." By utilizing vivid, often spectacular, imagery in the pageants, the "moral principles associated with the past" could be disseminated to an ever-wider audience.[97]

Though there were important exceptions, such as the IWW Pageant during a strike in Paterson, New Jersey, and a Suffrage Pageant in Washington, D.C., the majority of pageants during the Progressive Era were used by Anglo-American civic officials to bolster local community development. Pageants posited a glorious future out of an equally glorious past, a future, and a past that emphasized cohesion and harmony. Differences in class and ethnicity were nonexistent. In the more "pluralistic" pageants, different nationalities demonstrated their "folk ways" as contributions to a cosmopolitan America, but they eventually united "as Americans within the framework of a white, Anglo-Saxon Protestant nation." According to Glassberg, civic officials and reformers believed that such entertainment would "help heal potentially dangerous social antagonisms" and "revitalize the 'deep underlying communal affinities' that held their towns and cities together."[98]

The American Pageant Association published sample manuscripts and guides, and civic officials hired "outside experts" to write and direct their pageants. Pageants, therefore, were a kind of mass entertainment; they were publicized widely and audiences in different parts of the country could judge their own pageants by the standards of others. Consequently, though each town's local history was apparently different, their pageants were similar to each other in their images of the past, present, and future. According to Glassberg, these similarities in "historical images and ritual action" reflected a desire to promote "pious beliefs and virtuous behaviors, wholesome expressive recreation, local community cohesion, and a deep faith in orderly progress."[99]

Nearly every pageant contained scenes depicting settlement; encounters with Indians; the Civil War; communal festivities such as weddings, husking bees, and baptisms; and a symbolic "America" welcoming immigrants from different nations, though not, significantly, blacks or Asians.

Past generations were typically depicted as "religious, temperate, hard-working, and patriotic." Settlers overcame hardships such as disease and drought with an amazing stoicism. Contact with Indians was depicted as one of smooth transition rather than conflict. In wartime, settlers were patriotic, idealistic, and self-sacrificing. As with the Indians, social relations were presented as smooth and conflict-free. Indeed, pageant-masters advised civic officials to present nothing that could "arouse nascent class sentiment." Likewise, each immigrant group was accepted into the community without encountering open hostility or prejudice.[100]

In addition to these generic scenes, chronological time was crucial in the pageant. Each pageant typically began with the settlement of different nationalities and ended with a grand finale in which "America" or the "Spirit of the Community" cheerfully welcomed new immigrant groups. In the midst of the pageant, men participated in crucial economic and political changes in the community, while women tended to the "social and domestic side of community life." "Timeless events" such as church services, husking bees, and so on, represented "underlying emotional bonds of community," while weddings "represented the community re-producing itself from generation to generation." Social and technological changes were depicted in the context of a larger progressive history that was, according to Glassberg, almost an "organic process from forest primeval to 'City Beautiful.'" Any disparity between the past and the present appears within a larger narrative that "links" these disparities as "successive stages in the social and technological evolution of the town, leading to the fulfillment of local residents' sacred communal destiny." Any doubts about this evolutionary progress "are resolved in the grand finale, when all pageant participants, attired in historical costumes representing successive generations, confidently stride forward into the future."[101]

Such historical pageantry, Glassberg convincingly argues, paradoxically "promoted hierarchy, discipline, and rational organization" as a means to "achieve a celebration of democracy, spontaneity, and lyrical emotion." Pageant masters and civic officials presented towns, and sometimes cities, as "manageable arena[s] for reconstructing the intimacies of community while fostering loyalty to the nation, for asserting the essential continuity of local tradition in the midst of sweeping social and economic change."[102] Such a narrative structure served well the Norwegian-American Centennial organizers' purpose. Within the familiar pageant format, organizers could spectacularly demonstrate the Norwegian and Norwegian-American history that rendered them particularly able American citizens.

Indeed, *The Pageant of the Northmen* had a great deal in common with Anglo-American progressive pageants, a resemblance that helped to "anchor" the pageant's imagery within the organizers' conservative meaning.

Well aware of the pageant tradition, organizers hired an "outside expert," pageant master Willard Dillman, to write and direct their pageant. Before deciding on the pageant's final content, the pageant committee took suggestions from members of the community. For example, Alma Gutterson detailed the organizers' larger narrative when she wrote to the committee, suggesting that "the keynote of the pageant should be that men of Norse blood have those qualities that make for desirable American citizenship and that the earlier Norse immigrants not only conformed to American standards and ideals but were among the very people who created them." Gutterson suggested that the first half of the pageant depict early Norse exploration in the New World, followed by Columbus's "discovery" centuries later. Continuing the chronology would be the 1825 immigrants and a depiction of pioneer life in the Midwest and their "steady progress in prosperity." Gutterson interrupted her narrative to insist that the pageant present here some "item" demonstrating the "wholeheartedness with which Norse immigrants accepted and defended American ideals, customs, and standards." Such an item should "stress the fact that Norse immigrants did not and do not need to be 'assimilated,' but naturally do develop into sturdy, constructive, sane, loyal American citizens." Gutterson's pageant would end with scenes depicting "prominent Norsemen" as children, youth, and adults, recognizing their contributions to American society as a whole.[103]

Gutterson's suggestions squarely reflected the organizers' legitimating process and the stories so central to that process. Both the mythic Viking heritage and the history of sturdy pioneers were crucial to the organizers' representation of Norwegian-American ethnicity. In the final pageant manuscript, Dillman combined this narrative vision with familiar elements from Anglo-American pageantry. According to Glassberg, after World War I, when pageants were used to bolster loyalty drives, historical pageants lost their progressive, evolutionary vision of history. They still depicted "idealized behavior of past generations for present generations to emulate" and that history was "cohesive and free of discord." However, the past and the present were "less woven into a coherent story of successive stages."[104] The past appeared "fundamentally different from the present" and was depicted in discrete, self-contained episodes that were more nostalgic than dynamic stages leading inevitably to the present and into the future. This was not, however, true for the Norwegian-American pageant. It maintained an evolutionary vision of history that was crucial to the organizers' narrative.

The story of Hans Heg and his family, following heroically in the footsteps of those in both the Viking and the pioneer migrations, placed Norwegian Americans squarely in the immigrant and pioneer traditions as celebrated in many American civic pageants. The easy pluralism such a story promised was most forcefully imagined in a scene soon after the arrival of the Norwegians in Wisconsin and before the departure of the Indians. As the Indians and Norwegians mingled, three Americans in covered wagons entered on their way to Oregon or California. They stayed for the night and the "three nationalities" joined each other around a campfire. The audience watched as each group sang its own song and then all sang "Home Sweet Home," each group in its own language.[105] This scene was reminiscent of the pluralistic aspects of some Anglo-American pageantry in which each culture contributes its more "colorful" traditions to a unified Anglo-American cultural framework, in this case, each using its own language to sing the quintessentially American "Home Sweet Home."

The particular contributions of the Norwegians in America were solidified in the Civil War scenes and Colonel Heg's death after leading a regiment of Norwegian men. First, these scenes established that Norwegians fought valiantly and heroically for the preservation of the union. Their patriotism, particularly after the ambiguous experience of World War I, did not deserve to be questioned. Second, as with such scenes in Anglo-American pageants, the Civil War ultimately signified unity over diversity, community rather than conflict. Each of these meanings supported the organizers' representation of Norwegian Americans as loyal citizens whose values were compatible with American ideals, safe, and conflict-free. The finale was also in keeping with the rest of the celebration: the orations about Norwegian-American patriotism, piousness, ingenuity, and the exhibits depicting Norwegian-American progress in the arts and the professions. And it was conflict-free. There was nothing about Norwegian-American contributions to radical politics, about anything that would be perceived as a threat to 1920s American society. The similarities between *The Pageant of the Northmen* and the Anglo-American pageants—the generic scenes that would be recognizable to an audience—served, therefore, to reinforce the organizers' vision that Norwegian-American culture was compatible with American ideals.

In his memoir of the Centennial and events leading up to that celebration, Pedersen recounted a May 17 celebration of Norwegian independence, held in New York and attended by Norwegian visitors en route to the Centennial: "[The Norse American] is thrilled by the Sagas of his ancestral home, and he prides himself of his pioneer sires on this side of the sea. For that reason, his celebration lacked all that in any way can be termed political propaganda; he is attached to the Northland by the bonds of a common heritage of Saga and song."[106] Such an image was clearly the intention of those who organized the largest of several Norwegian-American celebrations that year. But, as one scholar of popular culture has recently argued, the invocation of the past to legitimate the present is "a precarious undertaking. . . . Tradition used to legitimate untraditional behavior may instead call attention to the disparity between the past and the present."[107] Anthropologists have taught us that symbols are not transparent "windows" onto a culture, but are "operators" in social processes. Some symbols serve to actually produce social transformations, to move "actors" from one status to another. Rites of passage are the most obvious example of this. At other times, particularly in terms of civic festivals, symbols serve less a transformative function than as a means of conforming, stating, and / or constructing identities. Within such a social process, symbols and ritual activity can be didactic; they can be displayed in such a way that they evoke a very specific message. At the same time, symbols are by their nature ambiguous, polyvalent, and therefore excellent vehicles for articulating contesting ideas.[108] On the one hand, the didactic display of symbolic objects and civic rituals at the Centennial celebration served to suspend internal conflict among the participants in favor of a particular construction of ethnic identity that represented Norwegian Americans as "safe" ethnics worthy of American acceptance. On the other hand, the ambiguity of those very same symbols and rituals speaks to a more complex and contested construction of Norwegian-American ethnicity. The next chapter will examine both the alternative visions of ethnic identity that did exist in the event as well as the instability of the organizers' middle-class narrative.

——— 5 ———

"The Nation's Only Safe Foundation":
Fields of Meaning
in an Ethnic Celebration

✦ ✦ ✦ ✦ ✦ ✦

In an early publicity letter to newspapers, Centennial Committee President Gisle Bothne asserted that the celebration would do for the Norwegian immigrants what a recent celebration at Plymouth Rock had done for descendants of the *Mayflower*. In this "never to be forgotten event," the "past will be clarified, the present will be intensified, and the future will be magnified." Bothne predicted that by the end of the four days, "tens of thousands of the present generation will have visualized the life of the early Norse pioneers, how they labored and sacrificed that we might gain wisdom and happiness and material comfort, and that we might lead such a life that Norway should not be ashamed of us, and America should not regret that she had invited us to her shores."

Bothne then likened the event to a Norwegian folk tale: "The Norse-American celebration will be like a river of living water, like Mimer's fountain of Norse mythology. Those who drank of this fountain received knowledge and wisdom. Odin himself, king of the Gods of Norse mythology, came and begged a draught of this water, which he received, but he had to leave one of his eyes in pawn for it." Bothne continued by inviting everyone to "come and drink of this fountain of entertainment, education, and inspiration. We feel sure that all who come will go away refreshed and happy, convinced that in the household of God the Norsemen are a peculiar people, vowing to be true to their highest ideals." He ended by assuring his audience that "instead of weakening their allegiance to America, the Centennial is certain to make all citizens of Norse blood or birth better Americans than ever before."[1]

In many ways, Bothne's letter is a clear example of the ideological legitimation that was at the center of the organizers' narrative construction of Norwegian-American ethnicity. His progressive rhetoric and his references to the *Mayflower* celebration placed the Norwegian celebration squarely within an American festive tradition. Bothne's other references, however, undermined this process of legitimation. His shift of focus to Norwegian mythology signified not only the important cultural and national roots of the celebration, but intimated loss and the pain involved in immigration in his comparison to Odin's loss of an eye in return for wisdom. Bothne ended with the claim that the Norwegians were a "peculiar" people whose very "peculiarity" would make them "better Americans than ever before." This rhetorical strategy challenged the popular notion of America as a homogenizing "melting pot" by undergirding his invocations to patriotism with a claim to peculiarity or difference. Furthermore, the graphic reference to Norwegian folklore signified that this was no easy resolution, but one borne of pain and loss.

Anthropologists often place festivals into two categories—oppositional or institutional. In general they are celebrations that "reaffirm" the cohesion of a social group. But, as Marianne Mesnil argues, the "dynamic nature of the carnivalesque festival is . . . a function of the relation between the reference group and the global society in power. It will be 're-bellious' (oppositional) in the first societal model (Bakhtin) and 'institutional' in the second model (Eliade), depending on whether the festival's community support is leveled with the power structure or against it."[2] The Centennial celebration, however, was both "institutional" and "rebellious." On one level, Bothne's statement is a clear example of the organizers' efforts at cultural legitimation. These middle-class organizers invoked the past to create a Norwegian-American identity that was compatible and nonthreatening to American culture and ideals. And such a strategy worked very well, as the last chapter demonstrates. No evidence is more convincing of this than Coolidge urging that Congress allow more Norwegians to emigrate. The organizers successfully set Norwegian Americans apart from the "unassimilable" southern and eastern Europeans. But according to anthropologist Allesandro Falassi, the ultimate meaning of festival is the community's "physical survival."[3] While the organizers disseminated a nonthreatening Norwegian Americanism, they presented this vision in terms of the survival of an *ethnic* community, which was itself a threat to the dominant ideology of assimilation and its necessity in an inevitable progression of American history.

On one important level, the celebratory symbols were carefully orchestrated by the middle-class organizers to express a Norwegian-American identity that was compatible with mainstream American culture. The apparent seamlessness of this narrative only signified more profoundly the deep need of these organizers to appear nonthreatening. But narratives are never seamless. They are parts of a continuous dialogic process between speakers and listeners, between present and past, between what is included in the narrative and what is excluded. The accumulated, often conflicting, experiences and desires of the community were present at the Centennial, confounding, in true celebratory form, any easy reading of this social text. While the organizers' purpose was to place the notion of "peculiarity" unequivocally within American goals and ideals, the very fact of these contradictions created the potential for oppositional interpretations of the event. Even though the organizers' "symbolic umbrella" provided a nonthreatening ethnic identity compatible with American ideals, it was held aloft by a powerful historical memory of Norwegian romantic nationalism. This romantic nationalism infused the references to Norwegian folklore and mythology telling of a heroic past and a uniquely democratic and law-abiding people as well as the intimate connections to Norway made through music, poetry, exhibits, and reunions. This history rendered the whole subject of Norwegian-American ethnicity highly unstable, equivocal, and contradictory. The instability and ambiguity of the symbolic objects and ritual events, as well as the presence of overtly alternative visions of Norwegian-American ethnicity, may have led participants to abandon the preferred reading of the organizers from either a negotiated or an oppositional interpretation based on their own experiences as ethnics in American society, a possibility that demonstrates the cultural contestation rooted within even seemingly conservative rituals.[4]

Bothne's words are significant here. In the context of a culture that sought to obliterate differences, his notion that Norwegians were a "peculiar" people resonates with the unresolved tensions about Norwegian-American ethnicity, tensions that the organizers were unable to contain. The very fact that the Norwegian-American community chose to celebrate its immigrant heritage at this historical moment is significant, for when a social group celebrates an event, it also "celebrates itself." In these events, the group "attempts to manifest, in symbolic form, what it conceives to be its essential life."[5] Or as Roger Abrahams argues, celebrations are "a time for giving and receiving the most vital emblems of culture in an unashamed display of produce, of the plenitude the community may boast." These emblems are dense with meaning "for they are invested with the accumulated energies and experiences of past practice."[6] Though Abrahams is speaking specifically here about agricultural celebrations, the Norwegian Americans at the Centennial certainly had their own display of "produce," as manifested in the material and spiritual success of Norwegians in America; Norwegian and immigrant crafts, heirlooms, art objects and inventions; souvenir medals, stamps, and postcards depicting both their Norwegian and American pasts; a display of Norwegian spirituality; a parade of "notable" Norwegian-Americans; ethnic music programs; and a large and extensive historical pageant. Yet these objects and practices signify more than the "produce" of the community; they exemplify the ways in which social life and ethnic identity become encoded in symbolic form.

Like all celebration, the Centennial was reflexive. In Turner's words, "if all principles and norms were consistent, and if all persons obeyed them, then culture and society would be unselfconscious and innocent, untroubled by doubt."[7] The Centennial occupied a "privileged" space in which the participants reflected upon their identities as Norwegian Americans. In this liminal space, Americanist rhetoric existed, not harmoniously, but in dynamic tension with Norwegian culture and history. As Turner has argued, we need "to discover the 'field' of meaning in which a celebratory object has its potential for arousing thought, emotion, and desire."[8] The context of the 1920s and the "threats" confronted by the organizers formed one "field of meaning" within which the Americanist symbols and rhetoric operated. Within this field, the organizers' larger narrative paralleled the progressive narrative of mainstream culture in its emphasis on expansion, individuality, and linearity. The context of Norwegian culture and history, on the other hand, formed another "field of meaning" that is crucial to understanding the complex meaning of the Centennial. Within this field, symbolic objects and events focused on literal, intimate, and communal connections to Norway. While the first served the dominant discourse of opportunity and power, the second served a countermemory of possibility and desire. It was this sense of possibility and desire that undercut the organizers' nonthreatening vision of ethnicity and created room for a world where ethnic memory actually opposed dominant American values of conformity and the inevitability of progress.

The rise of romantic nationalism in Norway in the mid-nineteenth century mirrored the rise of romantic nationalism in other European countries. Unlike the nationalism linked to Enlightenment ideals of a world community, romantic nationalism attempted "to redraw political boundaries to fit the contours of ethnic bodies." Such a nationalism linked popular sovereignty to the notion that each nationality was inherently and organically different from the others. In such a state, national consciousness built upon past traditions and myths, on folklore. German scholar Johann Gottfried Herder takes most credit for putting into words and disseminating this philosophy. Historical continuity was the first cornerstone of Herder's conception. The "fatherland," he argued, " 'has descended from our fathers; it arouses the remembrance of all the meritorious who went before us, and of all the worthy whose fathers we shall be.' "

Second, each historical epoch forms an organic whole that combine to create a unique, organic nation that "must be the master of its own destiny." This independent cultural entity, the nation, is largely determined by the physical landscape. This landscape, enhanced by historical movements and developments, evolves into distinct nations. According to Herder, the "national soul" reflects these organic structures. He wrote, " 'As a spring derives its flavor from the soil through which it flows, so the ancient characters of nations arose from family traits, from the climate, from the way of life and education, from the early transactions and deeds peculiar to them. The customs of the fathers took deep root and became the internal prototypes of the race.' " Herder argued against the Enlightenment hope of a common cultural community. If each nation did not develop its own national character, the native cultural forms—and, ultimately, the nation—would die.[9]

In 1882 Ernest Renan said, "Getting its history wrong is part of being a nation."[10] Stories about the past were crucial to nation-building and romantic nationalism. Herder and others argued that nations could "rediscover their lost souls" through folk poetry and folk tales, which they believed explained history and reflected the organic structures of the nation. Humanity could progress only if each nation contributed its unique character and cultural foundation. Patriots in central and eastern Europe sought to liberate their people from foreign domination by restoring national characteristics and cultural values embedded in folk stories and epics. Finland and Norway were also part of this movement. Norway and Denmark had been linked since 1397 in the Kalmar Union, originally a relationship of equal partners. Denmark, however, took a more powerful role in the union, and, at the Congress of Vienna after the Napoleonic Wars, Norway was given to Sweden to compensate for its loss of Finland. Despite Norway's attempt at becoming an independent, democratic nation when Norwegian leaders drafted a constitution at Eidsvoll in 1814, the Vienna treaty stood. Norway would not become independent until 1905. In the intervening years, Norwegian nationalism flourished.[11] By the mid-nineteenth century, a group of romantic nationalists, led by, among others, poet Bjornsterne Bjornson and playwright Henrik Ibsen, argued forcefully that Norwegians were not Scandinavians, but Norwegian, with a unique character and "soul." They believed that, for its salvation, the nation must turn to peasant traditions and folklore. Folk tales and Viking sagas were collected, published, and disseminated to an enthusiastic public.[12] Folk dances were performed in "traditional" costume and interest in folk crafts revived. Preservation societies were organized in the 1840s to capture what had not yet been lost. Intellectuals began a long process of "Norwegianizing" the language by infusing the Danish-influenced literary language with Norwegian vernacular. Ole Bull, an "infant prodigy violinist," popularized Norwegian folk music and introduced it to western Europe and America. Bull, in true romantic spirit, claimed "the mountains of Norway" taught him to play.[13] When Norway gained complete independence from Sweden in 1905, Norwegians in Norway and America played host to large and boisterous celebrations, rallying around the newest symbols of Norwegian cultural and political independence—the flag and the anthem.

In the context of a very recent and fervent romantic nationalism in Norway, the Centennial organizers' use of Norwegian folklore, mythology, and patriotic imagery signified much more than a historical compatibility with American culture. On the surface, the organizers' middle-class narrative paralleled—and legitimated—the dominant culture's Anglo-American progressive ideology. It is significant, however, that, though not widely advertised by the organizers, the opening day of the Centennial was the twentieth anniversary of Norwegian independence from Sweden. The powerful Norwegian nationalism in the celebration served to subvert this parallel and invert the hegemony of Americanization ideology. For Norway, not America, was the redemptive sacred space in both the organizers' vision and the alternative narratives present at the Centennial. In her speech about Martha Larsen, known as "the first lady of the *Restaurationen*," Hannah Larsen told her audience that, at eighty, her mother had exclaimed to a friend leaving for Norway, "I feel as if you were going to heaven!"[14] In recounting this small story, Larsen gave a literal voice to the concept of Norway as a sacred space, a space from which Norwegian Americans derived the characteristics with which they had contributed so mightily to American—and world—culture. In a speech to the Women's Missionary Federation of the Norwegian Lutheran Church immediately following the Centennial, Mrs. I. D. Ylvisaker told her audience that people "care so profoundly for the old things" because "they typify inner characteristics." She noted, "people are like trees—the tree sends its roots down, down to find the secret springs which sustain and give it life, and though the roots of some trees spread out and not down, every tree has a 'Hjerterod,' a heart-root, that goes straight down." So it is, she argued, with Norwegian Americans, who have "spread out" from Norway. "We send our roots down to find those secret springs, which have fed our lives during this century and made them what they are."[15]

In their analysis of W. E. B. Du Bois's progressive jeremiad, historians David W. Noble and David Howard-Pitney argue that in African-American tradition, "if America fails as a redemptive environment, Africa still remains as a source of purpose and meaning."[16] This was true also for many Norwegian Americans in terms of Norway. Just as Du Bois claimed that Ethiopian cultural and spiritual values could revitalize an America in declension, so did many Norwegian Americans argue that their heritage would make them better Americans and, therefore, make America a more just society. This sense of nationalism is the key to understanding the complex meaning of the Centennial celebration. Though nationalism was invoked by Norwegian Americans for some often divergent reasons, it nevertheless signified that Norwegian Americans were, as Bothne claimed, a "peculiar" people, a position that inverted and challenged the dominant "melting pot" ideal.

This sense of "peculiarity," or difference, formed the core notion of romantic nationalism, which argued that there is an organic relationship between history and the natural environment, a relationship most profoundly evident in the humble lives and heroic stories of the "folk." The most direct and explicitly outlined statement of romantic nationalism at the Centennial was O. E. Rolvaag's speech, delivered in Norwegian on June 8. Rolvaag had become one of the most outspoken proponents of Norwegian romantic nationalism in an American context. His profound belief in the need to preserve Norwegian culture in America linked directly to the rise of Norwegian nationalism. In both his public and his private writings, from the 1890s to his death in 1931, Rolvaag consistently reiterated his belief that a true American culture must invest in the native resources of its immigrants, who in turn must preserve their heritage or suffer a soulless life. As the term "soulless" implies, a cultural heritage was to Rolvaag—and to others who invoked nationalism—more than a surface layer of traditions. A cultural heritage made human beings human. As noted in previous chapters, his novels were filled with Norwegian immigrants who suffer great tragedy because they turn away from their Norwegian heritage.

Rolvaag's speech at the Centennial was based on his 1922 essay, *"Omkring Faedrearven,"* or "Reflections on Our Heritage." In this essay, he specifically outlined those values that were "organically" Norwegian and must be rekindled in an American context, much as they were "rekindled" by patriots in nineteenth-century Norway. Reflecting the core notion of romantic nationalism, Rolvaag argued that "dissimilarity is about the only similarity mankind has in common." According to Rolvaag, differences between nations were born of an organic relationship between the natural environment and a people's history, traditions, and "outlook on life." Like the nationalists before him, he believed that "each people has a contribution to make [to world culture], and it has made it on the basis of its ethnic traits." Norwegians received "certain talents and inclinations" in their "cradles," and Rolvaag argued, "these things that we received as an inheritance lie in the depths of our beings. We can't do anything about them. . . . the fact is simply this, we have them."[17]

In making his point, Rolvaag reminded his audience of the fairy tale hero, Espen Askeladd, who was forever venturing forth from his humble shack to rescue a princess or save a kingdom from trolls. Rolvaag noted that "whether Espen sets forth alone, or his brothers go with him, all carry some food from home. The home might be the ultimate in disgrace; still, there was something in it that had to be taken with them on their journey. How simple and beautiful the picture is. Isn't there always something from home that will nourish a man after he leaves?" Askeladd took this "something from home" with him into his battle with the trolls. Remarkably, continued Rolvaag, Askeladd "goes directly into the home of the trolls, lives with them, learns from them, coaxes secrets from them, takes of their riches, and at the same time remains human." The lesson, of course, was that the Norwegian, "wherever he wanders, whatever fate deals out to him," maintains "his most distinctive traits."[18]

Rolvaag believed that Norway's natural environment had created a people with a keen sense of place and a love of home. He argued that the Norwegian landscape was a "'first love'" that was "not easily forgotten" by the Norwegian immigrant, but would "bind him closely to his home community." Within this landscape, he argued, Norway's historical orientation to agriculture and rural life had bred a people who prized equality and radical democracy. At the same time, he believed that Norway's heroic history, as recounted in the Viking sagas and folk tales, had created a nation of independent and adventurous Askeladds who would carry Norwegian culture to the rest of the world. Each of these interacted and combined to create an independent, organic ethnic culture, which could be located and rekindled in folklore, mythology, and literature.[19]

Rolvaag's brand of nationalism contained an explicit critique of American culture. In the American context, he argued, the adventurous, questing spirit of the folk hero Askeladd had been lost. Norwegians in America were too cautious and calculating: "we figure and figure on what is possible; we calculate and count the cost." The materialism that had stopped America from moving forward had also stifled the Norwegian spirit, a spirit which, in Rolvaag's view, Norwegian Americans should rekindle and from which Americans should learn. For example, the Norwegian love of home and community, and the land on which both of these stand, explains why Norwegian immigrants don't remain in cities—"a home must be owned." For Rolvaag, the concept of "home" implies land, a family, and stability. He contrasts this with an American "boosterism" in which a home is a house and worthy of pride only if it has a high resale value. According to Rolvaag, while there are great "riches" in the Northwest, there are very few "real homes," which leads to part of the "spiritual poverty" he finds so prevalent among all Americans. There are places of "refuge, lodging," but there is a marked difference between these and a home. He cannot understand the buying and selling of houses. "One *builds* a home, or one inherits it from one's father. . . . *memories* and *traditions* are part of one's home." He laments the fact that Americans "are fast becoming a nation of movers and renters" because "genuine, true love of country cannot exist if there is no love for one's home. If the last is not present, the first remains nothing but gibberish and hysteria." Therefore, the Norwegians "must try to perpetuate the Nordic concept of home" to create a better America.[20]

Rolvaag's "concept of home" is closely related to his notion of the role of farming in Norway and America. Rolvaag believed that the Norwegian was "created for farming" and that, even under aristocratic governments, the Norwegian farmers always felt "themselves equal, as *human beings*, to the foremost man in the country." He notes that America at the time particularly needed that part of the Norwegian heritage. To prove this, he launches into a revealing discussion of the growing "rift between the wealthy and industrial workers." For Rolvaag, "both capital and labor seek all possible political influence"; the capitalist is ruthless and the working classes are too influenced by a radical socialism. Only the farmer stands outside of this dichotomy. He equates the Norwegian brand of socialism with American Progressivism to make his point. He asserts that in America, "things haven't turned out right in the last twenty years. Nor will things be 'all right' if we pray the prayer of the Pharisees, thanking God that we Americans are so much better than other peoples. We must teach ourselves to take well-intentioned criticism from whatever source it comes." One of the best "brakes" he can comprehend to stop "the trend of growing industrial slums, strikes, and radical socialism" is "a strong, well-informed farm population with a democratic feeling for *land-ownership, tradition, and home."* We must also glorify, "in speech and writing, country life over city life." He proposes that the government aid "people without means to make a home on as much arable land as is necessary for a livelihood. Such help would be a powerful antidote to socialism. Men who own the land they till do not readily become socialists."[21] This collapse of Norwegian ethnicity into political progressivism is a classic case of class politics being naturalized through appeals to blood ties.

After describing how Norwegians have an inborn reverence for law and order, an inordinate hunger for knowledge that is not being met by the American school system, and an innately religious nature, he focuses on the Norwegian passion for "individual freedom." Rolvaag notes that many outside his ethnic group comment on how well Norwegians become good Americans. But, he argues, "the Norwegian immigrant did not *become* good or indeed *become* American. He already *was* both before he emigrated, even as long ago as the age of the sagas." This is because at the "heart of American ideals" is individual freedom "under the law of the land." According to Rolvaag, "it is by no means impossible that this ideal, as well as many of America's free institutions, is part of an *ancient Norwegian heritage*." Rolvaag argues that America hasn't reached this ideal, though "jingoists" would argue affirmatively. However, there is an opposition to this "blind Americanism"—not the "revolutionaries" but "the quiet ones" who "pray 'in secret' that the kingdom of God in all its beauty may also soon come to earth in social and political life." The Norwegian *"passion and drive and will to work"* for the goal of personal freedom would "be a blessing for our new country in the days to come." He ends on a transcendent note: "It will be to our unfading glory if we continue to lead in the great procession of progress and do not hang back with the masses. Here we confront a seeming paradox: the best Norwegian is the finest American!"[22]

These last observations are reminiscent of the organizers' larger narrative, though Rolvaag's point was to critique the culture by which the organizers were so anxious to be accepted. On a deeper level, however, there may have been more compatibility than not between Rolvaag's view and the organizers' narrative. For the nationalism upon which the organizers' narrative depended undermined its middle-class business orientation, subverting and inverting the dominant assimilationist ideology. In his study of nationalism, George Mosse argues that romantic nationalism was a kind of secular religion that appealed to passion, emotion, and a need for symbolic order, senses that appeared lost in the midst of bourgeois materialism and the increasing industrialization of all aspects of life. Harking back to premodern symbols and myths in public festivals and civic monu-ments, nationalism was based not only on pragmatism but also on a spir-itual unity with the past. These myths and symbols, according to Mosse, signified a longing to escape the constraints of industrialism and to restore a sense of community.[23]

Although Mosse discusses nationalism in terms of the nation-state—a homeland—it is necessary to broaden our idea of the nation to include a sense of connectedness through time and space. In an American context, therefore, we can talk about African-American nationalism, Norwegian nationalism, and so on, in nationalist terms. Norwegian-American na-tionalism in 1925 was not the same as Norwegian nationalism in 1925, but it was a powerful construction, nonetheless, that provided a significant source of identification.

Nationalism could, of course, evoke different responses and be used for different purposes, as Rolvaag's speech demonstrates. Wefald, for exam-ple, argues that for Norwegian Americans involved in farmer and labor politics, the memory of a Norwegian cultural heritage was pivotal. Ac-cording to Wefald, the memory of community, economic self-sufficiency, cooperation, and compassion for the poor contradicted the American suc-cess myth and translated into radical reform activity in the upper Mid-west.[24] Likewise, Norwegian-American women involved in the suffrage and equal rights movements invoked a Norwegian cultural heritage. For example, in a suffrage speech reprinted in the Norse-American Centennial Daughters collection, Alma Gutterson argued, like other nationalists, that Norwegian landscape and history, as described in sagas and folk songs, created a people of unique independence, courage, and industry. Such characteristics, she argued, made total equality for women in Norway occur much more quickly than in other places.[25]

The irony, of course, is that romantic nationalism and its focus on "organically" ethnic traits could also nourish both racism and fascism. Norwegian-American nationalism was not immune to such possibilities. In making his point about the essential differences between nationalities and ethnic groups, for example, Rolvaag emphasized the rural traditions among Norwegians, which endowed them with an innate sense of equal-ity and democracy. Norwegians, Rolvaag argued, were *created* for farming. Irishmen, on the other hand, were "created for cities, because [they] can elbow [their] way forward in the crowd." And the Englishmen have a "practical business sense." Last, the southern Europeans, according to Rolvaag, were "better fitted for large industry" because they could "ex-ist crammed together with others in huge tenements, live from hand to mouth, and still be tolerably satisfied with [their] situation." Each, Rolvaag argued, "is as he is because of ethnic traits. To deny this is simple stupidity."[26] While Rolvaag's statements were made in the belief that each ethnic group fit organically, and happily, into a specific place in society, others applied a similar racism in an argument to forbid certain ethnic groups—that is, radicals—from "infiltrating" American society. For example, Axel Johanson of Seattle wrote to Centennial president Bothne, suggesting that the Centennial committee publicize and encourage pilgrimages to the Valhalla Mountains in Canada, whose thirty peaks were named after figures in Norse mythology. Such publicity, he argued, would acquaint Americans with Norse mythology, which would be particularly useful "in our time of strife and turmoil with threatening European propaganda." He continued, "Shall we not let the world know that our Thor with his Mjolner is ever fighting the Midgard Serpent whose coils shall not find mooring place on our shores? . . . Let the Norse American Centennial, in appreciation and as befitting token to our country, its government and the American flag, nominate their modern 'Thor' under whose banner the Viking descendants would rally and fight the Midgard Serpent, giving it no quarter."[27] Such racism lent itself easily to fascist beliefs. Bothne also received a letter from William Schaunau, publisher of *The American Nordic Aryan* of Portland, Oregon. Schaunau wanted to use the occasion of the Centennial to call Bothne's "attention to the enormous studies that are being made especially in Germany to reorganize AND FREE the Nordic Aryan people." He mentions particularly a young man named Hitler and was hopeful that, as "the Nordic (Aryan) feeling was very strong in Minnesota," the university students would make contact with student groups in Germany, "for there is much in the Aryan Youth Movement of Germany that should be transplanted to our shores FOR THE PROTECTION OF THE HOMES OF THE FUTURE."[28]

In his recent study of nations and nationalism, Hobsbawm argues that while nationalisms based on ethnic superiority were artificial inventions aimed at exclusion, nationalism also grew out of the French Revolution and its emphasis on "the common interest" as opposed to aristocratic privilege. Nationalism contains these two contradictory meanings and impulses. Both serve the elite of the nation-state at the same time that they appeal to the "hopes, needs, longings and interests of ordinary people."[29] These "needs and longings" can foster a xenophobic patriotism or a radical democratic notion of "the people." While Hobsbawm emphasizes the first as the most common—and destructive—form of nationalism, he acknowledges at least the possibility of the second.

Benedict Anderson compellingly argues that in order to understand the power of nationalism—its power to unite people for both constructive and destructive purposes—we must understand it as an "imagined community" whose unconnected members "live(s) the image of their communion."[30] Hobsbawm uses Anderson's term to emphasize the nation-state as built upon a false foundation of myth and invention. As he states in his introduction, "Nationalism requires too much belief in what is patently not so."[31] While Anderson would agree with this, he emphasizes the "imagined community" as a deep, human need for order and immortality. The stories we tell ourselves about ourselves may be false, but they are powerful and can be used for bad or good.

Like Mosse, Anderson examines the religious, cosmological elements of nationalism. It is crucial to remember, he notes, that the dawn of nationalism in the eighteenth century coincided with "the dusk of religious modes of thought," which were primarily concerned with "the links between the dead and the yet unborn, the mystery of regeneration . . . with continuity." Enlightenment rationality "brought its own modern darkness," requiring "a secular transformation of fatality into continuity, contingency into meaning." The idea of the nation, Anderson argues, was particularly suited to this transformation. He writes, "if nation-states are widely conceded to be 'new' and 'historical,' the nations to which they give political expression always loom out of an immemorial past, and still more important, glide into a limitless future. It is the magic of nationalism to turn chance into destiny."[32]

Central to this concept of nationhood is a modern conception of calendrical time, for the nation "is conceived as a solid community moving steadily down (or up) history." Various members of a nation may never meet one another, but they have "complete confidence in their steady, autonomous, simultaneous activity." This community is not only "solid," but "natural," as evidenced in the very language of nationalism. This language, Anderson notes, is a "vocabulary of kinship." The idioms of parentage or home both "denote something to which one is naturally tied" and is therefore "unchosen." Anderson argues that "precisely because such ties are not chosen, they have about them a halo of disinterestedness." Like a family, the nation is "the domain of disinterested love and solidarity."[33]

This concept of the nation as an imagined community, "as a deep, horizontal comradeship,"[34] unites the divergent uses of nationalism and provides an important context for understanding the contradictions in the Centennial organizers' conception of Norwegian-American ethnicity. On the one hand, organizers used Norwegian history and culture to argue a unique status and compatibility with American culture. But in the context of the nationalism upon which that narrative depended, key examples of that narrative deserve to be re-examined. While the history of pioneering ancestors and their contributions to the material growth of the Northwest was an important element of the celebration, references to Norway and Norwegian history were much more significant. As the organizers' narrative demonstrated repeatedly, immigrant contributions to America were dependent upon uniquely Norwegian characteristics. While these characteristics, as disseminated by the organizers, were not a threat to American culture, their dependence upon a Norwegian nationalism was. Norwegian nationalism competed with Americanism throughout the celebration, making much more contradictory the apparently seamless narrative of the organizers.

While the rhetoric of the various orations and history lessons presented by the organizers did not urge the maintenance of "Old World" values in a permanent Norwegian subculture, it was also not a language of assimilation. In true celebratory form, there was a great deal of recombination of old and new cultural patterns, rendering more complex meaning to the celebratory objects and events. In festive activity, symbols are often arrayed in antithetical pairs, or binary oppositions. In the Centennial, there was a constant binary play between Norwegian and American celebratory objects and events. From the incessant display of Norwegian and American flags, the Norwegian and English languages, and the Norwegian and American dignitaries to the very themes of the exhibits and cultural performances, this binary opposition permeated the Centennial.

This opposition was perhaps most visible to the historical record in downtown Minneapolis. As one reporter described the scene, "Streets brilliant with the blue cross of Norway intermingled with the Stars and Stripes greeted the visitors as they moved through the loop. Every store was bedecked with bunting, every block a new riot of color. Automobiles swathed in the national colors of the two countries added their touch of gayety to the holiday scene." Another reporter observed that "two of the department stores had their fronts half concealed behind rows of giant Norwegian and American flags, twenty to thirty feet long. Members of Norwegian singing societies, in brilliant costumes of their societies, added color to the crowds. . . . Cabbies hung 'Velkhommen' signs on their cars and learned enough Norwegian to encourage business." A Donaldson's ad promised that visitors could indulge in American consumerism while eating "special Norwegian dishes" and listening to Norwegian music in

Fig. 14: Crowds gathered for the parade on Nicollet Avenue in downtown Minneapolis. *Courtesy Minnesota Historical Society.*

Fig. 15: Group photograph of the *bygdelag* organization, *Nordlandslaget*, taken at the fairgrounds near a replica of a Viking ship. *Courtesy Norwegian-American Historical Society.*

the tearoom. Young women in Norwegian peasant costumes would serve as guides. Dayton's offered similar fare.[35]

On one level, these binary oppositions supported the organizers' attempt to link American and Norwegian ideals. In their business-oriented, middle-class narrative, these two cultures existed in harmony. This "exegetical," or didactic, meaning of the symbolic objects and events was interpreted by the organizers for the participants in press releases and speeches. But symbols are multivocal, and the patriotic rhetoric, therefore, must not be taken at face value. In his study of "working-class Americanism," Gary Gerstle argues that historians have ignored the complexities of the rhetoric of Americanism that arose in the 1920s and 1930s, assuming that such language "encouraged adjustment rather than rebellion, conformity rather than dissent." Thus, historians of the Norwegian-American experience argue that the patriotic Americanism so evident at the Centennial signified the increasing Americanization of the community. However, according to Gerstle, the invocation of Americanist ideals was much more contradictory and problematic. By the 1920s, the "unprecedented national emphasis" on 100 percent Americanism "force[d] virtually every group seriously interested in political power—groups as diverse as capitalists, socialists, ghettoized ethnics, and small-town fundamentalists—to couch their programs in the language of Americanism."[36] In an even broader sense, such rhetoric could be viewed as examples of what scholars of the public sphere term "alternative" or "counter" publics. Historian Mary Ryan, for example, examines the ways in which nineteenth-century women created alternative public lives as they were denied access to the "official" public by using the sanctioned "private" rhetoric of domesticity as a rationale for public activity that would eventually redefine the "official" public sphere.[37] Such findings give pause to an easy interpretation of the Centennial organizers' Americanist rhetoric and symbolic displays, particularly when we consider that important sense of Norwegian nationalism that competed with representations of Americanism. It is important to concede, of course, that having the debate framed over "Americanism" rather than over "justice" or "morality," for example, does a great deal to skew the outcome of that contestation along assimilationist lines.

A second look at the famous "living flag" is significant here, however. The "transformation" of the Norwegian into the American flag, accompanied by renditions of both national anthems, was of course a spectacle devised by the organizers to signify not only the "ease and willingness" with which Norwegians became American citizens, but also the compatibility of ideals that made that possible. This was not an unproblematic representation, however. Anderson argues that national flags and anthems create a sense of "simultaneity." In singing a national anthem, for example, "people wholly unknown to each other utter the same verse to the same melody." Such simultaneity is the "physical realization of the imagined community."[38] At the Centennial, with its constant juxtaposition of American and Norwegian patriotic symbols, there were two competing acts of "simultaneity." Mrs. Lee's words describing the spectacle, however, betray the unequal nature of these acts. She noted, you will remember, that the "familiar and beloved" Norwegian national anthem, only twenty years old and sung in Norwegian, was met "with a din of applause and cheers of approval."[39] The words "familiar and beloved" are not merely descriptive categories. "Familiar," derived from "family," evokes intimacy, something that we are accustomed to. In Anderson's terms, the familial language signifies "natural ties" to something "unchosen." That the anthem was sung in Norwegian is also important. In Anderson's words, "what the eye is to the lover . . . language . . . is to the patriot." Through language, "pasts are restored, fellowships are imagined, and futures dreamed."[40] Because the organizers wanted to reach a younger generation of Norwegian Americans and the larger American culture, they needed to conduct the majority of the celebration in English. In this context, those moments when the Norwegian language *was* used were all the more significant. While on the one hand the "living flag" supported the organizers' ideological position, the powerful sense of a destined, imagined community undermined its potentially assimilationist motives, offering a world in which ethnic memory and desire were paramount.

Intimate, "familial" links to Norway permeated the Centennial celebration, from the *bygdelag* reunions, musical events, and exhibits of heirlooms and memorabilia, to the reactions recorded by the press to these symbolic events and objects. Sunday, June 7, was the official opening of the celebration, but the fairgrounds opened June 6 for the annual reunion of *bygdelag*. The *bygdelag*, as we have seen, were social organizations made up of immigrants and their descendants from the same villages or districts of Norway, the first of nearly fifty having been organized in 1899. The annual meetings emphasized old-country dialects, regional foods, and folk traditions. On the eve of the Centennial, a journalist described the *bygdelag* for Minneapolis readers:

> Here is the plot: Here and there in the rocky, scenic communities of Norway, marked by a fjord or a lake or a mountain or whatnot, have been established longer than history relates—little towns. They have become great cities, many

of them, but, big or little, each is the center of a community, a county. Each of these groups is like a big family, more or less related. Sons and daughters of these groups, remembering always that they or their fathers came from Lille Hamar, Bergen, Trondhjem, Stavanger or elsewhere, have organized into "lags," or clans, scattered widely over the United States, but meeting annually in convention.[41]

Over forty thousand Norwegian Americans attended the thirty-six *bygdelag* reunions on Saturday.

Although there is no evidence that the organizers acted on his suggestion, one man wrote from Los Angeles, wondering if it "would be possible to lay out the Minnesota Fairgrounds like the map of Norway . . . so it would be easy for the many *'bygdelag'* to locate their friends." This need to reunite with Norwegian Americans from the same regions of Norway was a central purpose of the gatherings. As one reporter described it, "There was pride in the faces of the visitors as they recalled the daring of their ancestors who led the way in the *Restaurationen* a century ago, and happiness in the thousands of reunions among many who met for the first time in years friends of their earlier days in Norway."[42] Another reporter told his readers that the *bygdelag* reunions would be "a day of memories, when Norsemen of America will . . . prove to each other that home ties are unbreakable."[43]

These "home ties" were more than literal connections to friends and family, however. One woman, for example, wrote to the committee asking whether there would be a register of names for each *bygd* or *lag* because she "would like to meet people from parts of Norway where most of my relatives are still living."[44] Whether or not they were involved in *bygdelag* organizations, many Norwegian Americans felt a powerful connection to other Norwegian Americans descended from families of the same region. For example, F. Engbretsen, the Portland, Oregon, editor of *Sambaandet* (The Tie That Binds), wrote to Bothne to express his willingness to publicize the celebration. He added, "During my 32 years of residence in the United States, nearly all on the Pacific Coast, I have followed the career of your good self, one reason being that I was born at Frhald and knew the Bothnes' family quite well. . . ."[45] Such literal and figurative connections linked Norwegian Americans through both space and time to an imagined community.

The language of "ties" to another place, to "home," were prominent. In his memoir, for example, Carl Pedersen quoted a report in a Norwegian-language newspaper about a May 17 (Norwegian Independence Day) banquet held for Norwegian singers en route to the Twin Cities via New York.

The reporter commented, "We live on memories of the past. . . . They exist in our subconscious, and appear at longer or shorter intervals, as the case may be. . . . Though we be thousands of miles away from our native land, and even though the blue ocean separates between the old and the new homeland, yet, instinctively, something within reacts when we turn the calendar leaf to the 17th of May. Perhaps, we notice it even more because of our absence from the old home. Once more 'memories' assert themselves—happy sunlit memories from our childhood days, when we marched proudly to the stirring melodies of music and song." Judge T. O. Gilbert echoed these sentiments when at the Centennial he introduced dignitaries from Norway. "Norsemen of America love their adopted land . . . but they will never forget that 'there lies a land toward the eternal snow.' They are bound to 'Gamle Norge' [Old Norway] with strong bonds. . . ." Connections such as these could evoke powerful emotions. Pedersen quoted Otto Clausen's reactions to the Centennial performance of the Norwegian Student's Choir from Oslo, who "specialized" in Norwegian folk songs. Several thousand people watched the performance on June 7 and Clausen remembered this day "in particular." When the choir sang "Brudefarden," or "The Bridal Party," he observed, "the old familiar tune found its way to the hearts of the hearers. Tears that came were quickly brushed away by strong hands. . . ." But the popular songs that ended the program "released the fettered emotions." He continued, "I've seen a great deal in the line of demonstrations, but never anything to equal the experience of that memorable day."[46] This very sentimental discourse reveals more than nostalgic responses. It reveals, in Turner's terms, the "subjunctive mood" of cultural practice—contingency, desire, and possibility.[47]

This "subjunctive mood" was particularly evident in the exhibits collected by the women's auxiliary. The historical exhibit constructed by Knut Gjerset provided a powerful visual representation of the organizers' narrative, of a history compatible with Anglo-American Progressive history. But the displays of Norwegian objects and heirlooms—and the correspondence about their collection—bespeaks another history, a history of family ties and communal memories. In a telling letter to Caroline Storlie, Bertha Law Dahls suggested that there be "a special exhibit from the Viking period" that stressed "the home side of it": rooming, clothing, utensils, and so on. She particularly wanted to emphasize the Vikings' "saga method of carrying history to the people. . . ."[48] The "history" carried "to the people" through such exhibits was not progressive, but turned inward and backward toward intimate and familial ties, both literally and figuratively.

Fig. 16: Norwegian singers posed in costume in front of a log cabin replica on the fairgrounds. *Courtesy Minnesota Historical Society.*

Chairs in each organized state located Norwegian Americans and amassed a rich collection of exhibit materials. They collected handmade wooden bowls, churns, an old pair of glasses, a chest made in 1727, Norwegian national costumes, an embroidered wedding shawl that belonged to one elderly woman's mother, needlework, among the many heirlooms. Some wrote to the committee themselves with donations. One woman, for example, asked if the committee could use a linen tablecloth made in Norway in the 1860s. "The flax," she wrote, "was raised on my father's farm, and all the work of making the finished article was done on the homeplace. . . ."[49] Annalia Winger wrote that she was not well enough to attend the Centennial, but she wanted to contribute several family heirlooms to a permanent Norwegian exhibit. "If I had children," she wrote, "I would not part with them, but as it is I would like to place them in an exhibit of Norse articles."[50] Ragna Grimsby from Montana offered a pin presented to her in 1915 by a Norwegian society in recognition of her act of bravery in saving a little boy from drowning. The pin was the first of its kind presented to an American, according to Grimsby. She also offered "the Sigvold Qvale *Gold Medal* that was won in the *very first* national declamatory contest in 1912. The declamation that won it was Bjornson's 'Bergliot.' "[51] Donations numbered from one item, such as a "Coffee Pot kept for seven generations," to twenty-five or thirty items. One collection included a full spectrum, from such mundane things as a "Pair of Curtain

In the North lies our beautiful Saga land
  In the arms of the god of the sea;
There the sun glows red in the noon of night;
There, thousand-hued, the northern light
  Gleams weird over fjord and lea!

I am longing to roam in that beautiful land—
  Dear land where my fathers have dwelt!
And feel the inspiring breezes blow
From cloud-like cliffs of eternal snow,
  My mother in childhood felt.

I am longing to hear the tinkling bells
  And the shepherd's clarion call
Ring o'er the tarns, the falls and the rills,
Ring o'er the woods, the vales and the hills
  And away to the mountains tall.

Fig. 17: Title page of the Centennial's souvenir program. *Courtesy Norwegian-American Historical Society.*

Hold-Backs" to a "Silver Goblet with Inscription, 'From King Carl Johan to Lasse Lassesen Glesness, Mar 11, 1842.' "[52]

Such examples tell us what these Norwegian Americans valued. These objects signified home, family, and community—in and with Norway. Indeed, these objects were valued so greatly that many expressed concern over their well-being. Organizer Camella Hardy noted that the people in her community were "quite concerned about the assurance of getting their items back."[53] Another organizer cautioned the committee that her contacts likewise wanted a guarantee for the safe return of their articles. "They all say the same thing. 'If I was sure to get it back, as I wouldn't want to lose it for any amount of money. . . .' "[54] These objects were valued not only because they signified connections to family, history, and Norway, however. They were also valued because they signified the owner's "Norwegianess." Perhaps the most poignant example of this was the letter to Storlie from Anna D. Parker, who immigrated as a child on the *Restaurationen*. She forwarded a story about the emigrant ship and her family, enclosing with it a lock of blond hair, which is still taped to the letter. The hair, she wrote, is from her youth, to "show you I had the typical Norwegian hair."[55] A woman from South Dakota sent a needlepointed cushion top for the exhibit, adding, "I am a real Norwegian myself and would love to have my work exhibited at the fair. . . ."[56] A Minneapolis woman listed for the committee her "Norwegian" credentials: "I have a mother 88 years came from Norway, Oslo—in 1869 been here ever since is well-known, best of health. I also have boy and girl twins born on 17th May [Norwegian Independence Day]—17 years old now. . . ." She ended her brief note by asking, "Where do I come in on this celebration of the Centennial? I like to do my share. . . ."[57]

These humble statements speak to the profound importance of Norwegian connections—to Norway, its history, and its people. One reporter described the scene in the exhibit building: "Past the relics of early days, the things that made homes for the early Norwegian pioneers, pushed all day long a never-ending stream of the pioneers' descendants. They stopped to talk, in Norwegian or English, over the needlework, the patchwork quilts and yards of fancywork, calling to each other: 'Remember Olga, grandma had a spread just like that one, only the flowers were purple. . . .' " The reporter, however, noted that what "typified the whole display" was the model farm exhibit, from the humble log cabin in 1886 to the modern farm with automobile, electric lights, and telephone.[58] This progressive display, however, stood not in harmony but in dynamic tension with the concrete, tangible objects that evoked a literal and figurative community of Norwegians.

Such a dynamic tension between the organizers' progressive narrative and an "imagined community" rooted in Norwegian nationalism was particularly evident in the souvenir program. Like the model farm exhibit, the program served well the organizers' overt purposes. President Bothne's foreword is juxtaposed to a photograph of Abraham Lincoln, titled "The Typical American." Following are photographs of the committees, President and Mrs. Coolidge, the Canadian and Norwegian royal families, and a Bible brought to America on the sloop in 1825. These visual images are followed by essays, articles on Norwegian-American politicians, a retelling of the migration story, a list of Norwegian Americans in public service, a chronology of events, and a series of advertisements by local businesses, each praising the Norwegians for their good citizenship. The organizers' preferred reading of this text was that these separate histories were compatible and, indeed, beneficial to the continued growth of American culture and society.

Embedded in this "safe" text, however, was a Norwegian nationalism that subverted this reading and inverted the dominant Americanization narrative. On the title page, this poem accompanies a pencil drawing of the sloop:

> *In the North lies our beautiful Saga land,*
> *In the arms of the god of the sea;*
> *There the sun glows red in the noon of night;*
> *There, thousand-hued, the northern light*
> *Gleams weird over fjord and lea!*
>
> *I am longing to roam in that beautiful land—*
> *Dear land where my fathers have dwelt!*
> *And feel the inspiring breezes blow*
> *From could-like cliffs of eternal snow,*
> *My mother in childhood felt.*
>
> *I am longing to hear the tinkling bells*
> *And the shepherd's clarion call*
> *Ring o'er the tarns, the falls and the rills,*
> *Ring o'er the woods, the vales and the hills*
> *And away to the mountains tall.*[59]

It is significant that the organizers chose this specific poem to display on the title page. The committee received a number of poems from Norwegian Americans that would have unequivocally served their purposes. Each began with romantic descriptions of the Norwegian landscape and mythological references, and each ended by recounting Norwegian contributions to America and stating loyalty to their "adopted" country. The organizers' choice, however, points to the contradictory and equivocal nature of their narrative. Though the anonymous poem is written from an immigrant's point of view, it is reminiscent of Bjornson's romantic nationalist poetry. The language of family and landscape intertwine to evoke the "unbreakable ties" that were so evident in the *bygdelag* reunions and the exhibits. As powerful components of nationalism, landscape and history combine to form an organic whole. In the textual construction of the program, everything follows this poem. Norwegian history in America, no matter how "safe" or nonthreatening, was dependent upon this link to Norwegian nationalism.

This link was represented both visually and textually. For example, in the essay that told the history of Norwegian Americans in public service, photographs of these governors and congressmen are, in rotogravure fashion, superimposed upon drawings of Norwegian mountains, fjords, and villages. In another historical essay, O. M. Norlie begins by quoting the patriot poet Bjornson:

> There lies a fair land 'neath the old glacial snow,
> There spring-life we find but in the narrow cleft low;
> The ocean rolls on with its saga roar,—
> Than this land no mother can loved be more.

Using history, geography, and mythology as references, Norlie then recounts the distinct characteristics of the Norwegian people. Mirroring Rolvaag's account, Norwegians are, according to Norlie, hardy, intelligent, highly moral, religious, hospitable, thrifty, independent, and radically democratic.[60] As we have already seen, the organizers used such a narrative to claim compatibility with American ideals. But it was not merely a compatibility. As the organizers demonstrated repeatedly, Norwegians had centuries earlier laid the groundwork for the very values considered "uniquely" American. While on one level this worked to the organizers' advantage in terms of creating a nonthreatening ethnic identity, it also handily subverted the whole concept of American exceptionalism.

The souvenir medal was the most powerful visual representation of this contradiction. Sold at the Centennial and pictured in the souvenir program, the medal provided the most potent imagery of the Viking heritage, signifying on the one hand that the very values purported to be typically

"American" could be traced to Norwegian culture. Norwegians were, therefore, "naturally" good Americans. The choice of a Viking over an immigrant as a visual representation for the *Centennial* is significant, however, for the Viking "discovered" not an already formed American culture, but an apparently empty continent. Not only did this subvert American exceptionalism, but it was also a willful insistence on the *uniqueness* of Norwegian immigrants among a nation of immigrants.

Norlie ended his essay by noting, like Bothne and Rolvaag, that "every nation is a peculiar people, called by God to perform a peculiar service for mankind."[61] "Peculiarity," or difference, was the core idea of romantic nationalism and the core contradiction in the organizers' narrative. Their vision of a "safe" ethnicity hinged on Norwegian Americans as a unique, "peculiar" people. This was a basic and profound challenge to American conformity and the forces of Americanization in the 1920s. Nowhere is this more evident than in the prize-winning essay in the organizers' contest, "Why We Celebrate."

Nine essays were submitted to the contest, and there was most disagreement among the judges over Norlie's essay, which they awarded second prize. The president of Augsburg College, a judge, charged that Norlie's essay "makes some bad errors, e.g. that no Norse men have served on the Board of Education for the city of Minneapolis, and charges that the community is prejudiced against the 'foreigners'. This is an unpardonable error, which excludes the essay from consideration." He noted also that "there is a certain animus, too, which I think is wrong and which will do us more harm than good." In a letter to Bothne, Norlie disagreed with the judge's assessment. He pointed out that one Norwegian American "was on the school board for a number of years and filled the schools with Norwegian janitors, not teachers. We were not good enough for teaching positions." Nevertheless, Norlie's essay was awarded second prize and printed in the program, though without the reference concerning the school board. Included, however, was a paragraph addressing prejudice against Norwegians by the larger culture. "The fact is," Norlie writes, "that in the past, and even at the present time, many of the so-called Americans, especially those of British ancestry, do not seem to know, or want to know, that the Norwegians are of their race, or that they have as good a right to be called Americans as anybody else, or that they are entitled to the same opportunities as their Anglo-Saxon brothers. The Centennial ought to secure from these good neighbors a more just recognition of what Norwegian really is."[62] While the controversy over Norlie's essay illuminates the tension within the community itself over Americanization, the revision served the organizers' ideological purpose by claiming an equal status for Norwegians with the Anglo-Saxon dominant culture.

Norlie, however, ended his essay with the notion of "peculiarity," significant in light of Falassi's argument that competitions are important elements of celebrations because "by singling out its outstanding members and giving them prizes, the group implicitly reaffirms some of its most important values."[63] The importance of "peculiarity" or difference was stated most powerfully in Waldemar Ager's first-prize essay. The essay, written by one of the most fervent anti-assimilationists in the community, was uniformly supported by the judges. In light of the organizers' larger narrative that sought to appease hostilities to difference, Ager's essay is remarkable. In the essay, Ager argued that one result of the Centennial would be to make Norwegian Americans feel that they have a common history with other immigrants, a history that had been left largely unwritten. The second and most important result would be a broader picture of American history built *together* by *different* people. In light of this, the "melting pot" is not a useful concept, according to Ager, for "a standardized citizen-type can only happen by exterminating the immigrants' strongest and best characteristics." For without this preservation, there is no "real folk soul." If this is lost, only an organism remains, for the "folk soul" gives life "color and intensity." Without it, he concluded, even "the richest home and the most powerful country would be impoverished." The Centennial would prevent this impoverishment because Americans would realize that ethnic strength, rather than conformity, is the "nation's only safe foundation."[64]

This prize-winning essay was steeped in romantic nationalism. Also, it was the only contribution printed in Norwegian, which served Ager's point only more powerfully. This was a key space in the Centennial, from which the significance of being ethnic, of being inextricably bound to a particular history, place, and people burst forth, rendering the organizers' conservative project profoundly contradictory and equivocal. In his speech at the Centennial, delivered in Norwegian in a session chaired by Ager, Rolvaag echoed the ideas in Ager's essay. He criticized his Norwegian-American audience for their tendency to use American jingoism. "Of course we are Americans," he argued, "and nothing but Americans—as citizens! . . . But by descent, by origin, by *family* we are Norwegians, and can never be anything else no matter how desperately some of us try."[65] For both Ager and Rolvaag, the concept of "soul" and "soulessness" was crucial. In their romantic nationalist philosophy, the soul is the embodiment of a nation's peculiar and unique history, landscape, and people, in other words, the repository of national or ethnic identity. Six years later, in his last novel, Rolvaag would tell his readers,

> A People that has lost its traditions is doomed! . . . One thing I see clearly: If this process of leveling down, of making everybody alike by blotting out all differences is allowed to continue, America is doomed to become the most impoverished land spiritually on the face of the earth; out of our highly praised melting pot will come a dull, smug complacency, barren of all creative thought and effort. Soon we will have reached the perfect democracy of barrenness.[66]

This powerful statement is reminiscent of Ager's Centennial essay, and both resemble a scene from Ibsen's *Peer Gynt*. When the Troll King demands that Peer give up his human identity, Button Molder melts down Peer's soul to forge a new soul that bears no trace of the original.[67] For Rolvaag and Ager, ethnic differences made human beings human.

Both Rolvaag and Ager spoke and wrote in the language of romantic nationalism about family, destiny, and an imagined community. Theirs were strong statements that gave form to the more defuse examples of nationalism in the reunions, exhibits, public reports, and correspondence. They also illuminated the contradictions in the organizers' narrative. Clearly, as noted, the main narrative presented by the organizers paralleled the dominant Anglo-Saxon narrative of discovery and progression. At the same time, however, it inverted the dominant narrative of conformity to uniquely American ideals. Both organizers and participants had to negotiate these contradictions in the struggle for meaning at the Centennial. Turner argues that "celebration may be said partly to bring about a temporary reconciliation among conflicting members of a single community. Conflict is held in abeyance in the period of ritualized action."[68] While bringing together dissenting members of the community under their "symbolic umbrella" was one of the organizers' goals, they tried to defuse any possible dissension by excluding from the start those members involved in radical politics. Nevertheless, they were unable to contain the contradictions within their own ideology. What united the diverse voices that did exist was the nationalism filtering throughout the celebration and the "imagined community" evoked by that nationalism.

As one of the most sensitive critics of Mikhail Bakhtin's theory of Carnival points out, celebration inserts into community and language structures "an indeterminacy, a certain semantic open-endedness, a living contact with unfinished, still-evolving contemporary reality."[69] While the civic rituals performed at the Centennial had very little of the peasant carnivalesque, Bakhtin's insights about celebration in general are nonetheless an important reminder of the open-endedness of public festivity. Centennial organizers and participants exploited that indeterminacy. At the same time that the dominant power structures were attempting to "fix social reality" in terms of Americanization, Centennial-goers were participating in a "countervailing" process by which, as Sally Falk Moore argues, people "arrange their immediate situations (and / or express their feelings and conceptions) by exploiting the indeterminacies in the situation, or by generating indeterminacies, or by reinterpreting or redefining the rules and relationships."[70] By manipulating the contradictions in their lives as ethnic Americans in the early twentieth century, Norwegian Americans were constructing their own version of social reality, a construction grounded in their social experience and the politics of culture. Furthermore, the organizers themselves were attempting to "fix social reality" in a way that made Norwegian-American ethnicity "safe" for American culture, business, and politics. But the contradictions implicit in their ideological position and the positions they were unable to contain made their effort indeterminate. The Centennial, then, is not the end of Norwegian-American history, as some historians would have it, but part of a continuing debate between the ethnic group and the dominant culture and within the ethnic group itself.

As Michael Bristol points out in his discussion of Bakhtin, Carnival is not a meaning in and of itself, "nor is it limited to any single social function, whether protest, accommodation, or cathartic release. It is primarily a language. . . ."[71] By viewing the Centennial as an open-ended dialogue, we can speak of it in broader terms through Bakhtin's dialogic theory of active reception. For Bakhtin, "every utterance is a 'two-sided act', 'the product of the reciprocal relationship between addresser and addressee' " which should always be thought of in context.[72] The dialogue between the Centennial and its participants took place in the context of the specific historical and social experiences of the Norwegian community, a dialogue that informed the dense meanings of the celebratory objects and events in the festival. Implicit in cultural practice is a struggle over meaning. The contradictions implicit in this celebration left it open to different interpretations by the organizers and the participants. The "language" of the Centennial was part of an ongoing and complex statement about and construction of Norwegian-American ethnicity. It was both accommodationist and resistant. This contradictory discourse was nowhere more evident than in the Centennial's culminating event, *The Pageant of the Northmen*.

As discussed in the last chapter, many of the pageant elements reinforced the organizers' narrative vision of a conflict-free ethnicity. At the same time, however, the very presentation of Norwegian-American mythical history and its connection to the present generation—a connection undergirded by romantic Norwegian nationalism—implicitly undercut and rendered unstable the organizers' conservative narrative. Furthermore, though this pageant was very similar to Anglo-American pageants, there were significant differences that further bolstered the organizers' claim to a unique status in American history at the same time that they undercut and subverted their attempt to appear safe and nonthreatening.

Chronological time was a key difference between the Norwegian-American pageant and other pageants of the era. Rather than beginning with settlement in the New World, the Norwegian-American pageant included the immigrants' earlier life in Norway. In the Progressive-Era pageants, the Old World is important only for the immigrants it contributes to an American "melting pot." In the Norwegian-American pageant, however, Norway is crucial. Historical time—the years, for example, immediately before the Hegs' emigration—is augmented by mythical time, which is remembered in the legends of the Vikings and the Christianizing kings, and in the folk tales and dances that offer a timeless sense of history and connection.

In one interesting sense, these scenes parallel the maypole dances and "merrie old England" scenes in Anglo-American historical pageants. In these pageants, particularly in the late nineteenth century, Anglos, too, tried to establish ethnic roots. The pageant images at the Centennial, however, were "anchored" by the historically specific "text" preceding them throughout the celebration. As previously noted, this "text" invoked the Viking age to demonstrate that Norwegians held a unique place in the age of exploration and that Norwegian values deeply affected the history of western Europe and, consequently, America. This "claim to status" was in many ways compatible with American ideals of discovery, individualism, and linearity. Within the progressive, evolutionary pageant format, this history and the values it invoked were present in the pioneers and, by extension, in the contemporary Norwegian-American community that was contributing so much to American society.

Nationalistic images provide insight into the complex nature of the pageant and of Norwegian-American identities. Romantic nationalism, with its empowering notions of peculiarity and uniqueness, encouraged Norwegian Americans to proclaim themselves "good" Americans. Nevertheless, that very uniqueness undermined Americanization ideology. Significantly, the pageant ended not with a symbolic "America" welcoming the nations of the world to a unified culture, but with a representation of *Norwegian-American* progress in the New World.

Although the pageant did not overtly critique American culture for its insistence on homogeneity and conformity, the sense of historical time in the pageant is an insistence on difference and peculiarity. The use of Viking history, for example, turned the organizers' narrative back on itself. Norwegian Americans were not just equally good Americans, they were better than other Americans because their ancestors had centuries earlier laid the foundations for so-called American ideals. While this story may have paralleled Anglo-American linear history, the folk tales and legends told to Hans bespeak a much more intimate, circular vision of history and memory. While Colonel Heg's activities in the Civil War supported the organizers' effort to demonstrate the excellent patriotic citizenship of Norwegian Americans, the very values that made his martyrdom possible came not from his contact with American culture but from his historical connection to the Norwegian mythical past. Heg had the will and determination of the Vikings and the sense of democracy and fairness of his more recent ancestors. Just as these stories linked Heg to an organic, heroic Norwegian past, the statue of Heg unveiled at the end of the pageant would connect contemporary Norwegian Americans through Heg to that same past—not an American past, but a Norwegian past.

Such a willful insistence on difference gives pause to any easy interpretation of the other pageant elements. For instance, in Anglo-American progressive pageants, community celebrations such as weddings and baptisms signified the reproduction of an Anglo-American culture. In the context of the alternative sense of chronological time in the Norwegian-American pageant, these same scenes—accompanied by Norwegian folk music and religious services—may have instead signified the reproduction and perpetuation of a "distinctly" Norwegian-American culture. The characters from the folklore stories told to Hans at his family's knee danced in the background throughout the pageant, reminding the audience that these intimate ties with Norway—through space and through time—could not be broken.

Perhaps the most telling scene in the pageant, however, was that depicting the immigrants' contact with the Indians. Throughout the Indians' preparations for departure and for a number of weeks following, their medicine man stood motionless on a rock. He watched his tribe leave and he watched the immigrants build a cabin and greet the group of newcomers. When two men finally approached the lone Indian, he indicated that though his people were all gone, "he hesitates to break away from the land where his forefathers were buried." According to the directions, "he then walked sadly in the track of his people and passed out of the picture."[73] This powerful scene signifies not so much an empathy for the Native American people as a metaphor for the pain involved in emigration, in leaving one's people. It is significant that the lone Indian was not a young boy who might be homesick, but a medicine man, whose wisdom concerning his situation could not be disputed. This scene, in the context of the Centennial and its contested vision of Norwegian-American ethnicity, would remind the audience that emigration, and being ethnic, was no easy task, but one borne of pain, struggle, and loss. Like the exhibits of memorabilia, Bothne's folkloric reference to loss in exchange for knowledge, and Rolvaag's insistence on taking a piece of home with one to remain fully human, this scene reminds us of Michael Fischer's argument that ethnicity is dynamic and "emerges in full" only "through struggle."[74] In these moments the supposed "uniqueness" of Norwegian Americans became an important alternative to the Americanizing rhetoric so prevalent at the celebration.

Like the progressive pageants, the Norwegian-American drama displayed an evolutionary, inevitable history in which the past informs the present and, by extension, the future. That past is not an American past, however, but a Norwegian past. In the finale, all of the characters from nearly a thousand years of Norwegian history formed an organic link through Heg to the present. The Norwegian-American pageant took a form normally used to disseminate an American nationalism to demonstrate that Heg's martyrdom was not due to an inevitable awakening to so-called American ideals, but to a natural progression from the ideals he learned through Norwegian folklore and mythology at his mother's knee.

Such a vision of history is particularly compelling given the immediate context of public displays of history in the 1920s. According to Glassberg, during this period, patriotic and hereditary societies "believed that the times required them to create and maintain permanent institutions dedicated to the preservation of items they identified with the purity of their Anglo-American heritage, rather than to join in activities such as community historical pageants that would merge that heritage with those of other classes and ethnic groups in the projection of a common present and future."[75] In this context, Norwegian Americans presented a pageant that celebrated a "peculiar" and distinct heritage, arguing that not only were Norwegians entitled to equal status in the culture with "Yankee" Americans, but also were actually *better* Americans based on the Viking founding story. Norwegian Americans posed a direct challenge to the Anglo-Saxon superiority that was enjoying not only a resurgence but a retrenchment.

Viewed in this context, the pageant may have had more in common with

W. E. B. Du Bois's answer to Anglo-American progressive pageants than the progressive pageants themselves. Reacting to the fact that progressive pageants left out black Americans except for scenes of slaves rescued by white Civil War soldiers, Du Bois in 1913 wrote and produced *The Star of Ethiopia,* a black history pageant commemorating the fiftieth anniversary of the Emancipation Proclamation. Performed in 1913, 1915, and 1916—and revived, significantly, in 1925—the pageant depicted five eras in African and American history. Like the Norwegian-American pageant, this drama did not begin with "settlement," that is, slavery, but with the black discovery of iron in prehistoric times. Du Bois recounts the growth of African civilization in Egypt and central Africa until just before European contact. The pageant then shifts its attention to America and the " 'Valley of Humiliation,' " slavery. The cruelties of slavery are represented against a background of spirituals and briefly interrupted with "a lively Creole dance." As a symbolic "Ethiopia" slowly awakens, freedom struggles increase. Scenes depicting Nat Turner, Frederick Douglass, and John Brown conclude with the exploits of Toussaint-Louverture and "the Haitian national anthem swelling in the background." As a chorus sings "The Battle Hymn of the Republic," black Union soldiers march across stage. The finale, depicting black progress since emancipation, consists of a procession of black ministers, physicians, athletes, and teachers who "overcome the 'Furies' of race prejudice, idleness, and intemperance to build a 'Tower of Light' out of the 'Foundation Stones of Knowledge.' "[76]

There were, of course, some significant differences between the Norwegian-American pageant and Du Bois's drama. A central feature of *The Star of Ethiopia* was the black struggle against slavery and racism. Blacks, unlike members of European ethnic groups, were never included in Anglo-American visions of a unified community. Such a central, overt conflict concerning ethnicity and Americanization was absent from *The Pageant of the Northmen.* The similarities, however, illuminate a common insistence on a crucial, distinctive, organic history and an insistence on a voice to disseminate that history to their respective communities and to the larger culture. For the Norwegian Americans, such a history proclaimed a status at least equal to Anglo-Americans. In that sense, it paralleled dominant American expansionist and progressive ideals. But the *distinctive* history—naturalized by nationalist ideology—on which those ideals were based in Norwegian-American culture, inverted the dominant Americanization narrative, leaving room for alternative visions of history and ethnicity.

Conclusion

Historical Memory and Ethnicity

✚ ✚ ✚ ✚ ✚ ✚

The pageant finale, with its unveiling of a Civil War hero preceded by a parade of "successful" Norwegian Americans from every profession, is emblematic of the conservative nature of the Centennial celebration. But there were other stories told at the Centennial that are emblematic of the contingent nature of that same celebration. President Bothne's powerful reference to Norse mythology—leaving one's eyes (one's subjectivity, one's ability to understand) for a drink of magic water (material wealth)— speaks to the profound costs of emigration. Indeed, Rolvaag argued that one cannot remain human while acquiring wealth if one does not take a piece of home—of culture, values, and ideals—when leaving. Such contradictory stories competed with each other within the Centennial's larger construction of Norwegian-American ethnicity. In his powerful words on historical memory, cultural critic Walter Benjamin argues,

> To articulate the past historically does not mean to recognize it "the way it really was." It means to seize hold of a memory as it flashes up at a moment of danger. Historical materialism wishes to retain that image of the past which unexpectedly appears to man singled out by history at a moment of danger. The danger affects both the content of the tradition and its receivers. The same threat hangs over both: that of becoming a tool for the ruling classes. In every era the attempt must be made anew to wrest tradition away from a conformism that is about to overpower it.[1]

The Norse-American Centennial was not indicative of an inevitable assimilation process from a static Norwegian "folk" culture to "100% Americanism," but was a complex dialogue at a historical "moment of danger" within the Norwegian-American community. Their reinvention of dominant American history to integrally include Norwegian ideals and virtues may be seen as an "attempt to wrest tradition" from the prevailing urge to conformism that wished to overpower it. To "read" ethnicity only in terms of static models of culture, assimilation, and hegemony is to miss the profound struggle over meaning in cultural practice and the continuous attempt to create and re-create ethnic identities.

The "moment of danger," however, did not merely pose a monolithic Norwegian-American community against the "ruling classes," the dominant Anglo-American culture. As the long-standing debates in the community demonstrate, Norwegian-Americans were not of one mind about the efficacy of Americanization, or about any political issue. Contrary to the narratives constructed by historians of the Norwegian-American experience, at no time was there an "authentic" Norwegian-American culture that was replaced by a unified American culture. The national drive to Americanize the immigrants fanned the fires of a long-standing debate within the Norwegian-American community itself over the extent of loyalty an ethnic should show his or her country. Though wartime nativism gave it a new immediacy, this process of dialogue and debate had been going on long before 1914. From at least the 1870s, families, workers, farmers, politicians, business leaders, church leaders, and members of ethnic organizations engaged in both private and public dialogues over language, politics, education, and Americanization. Artists, intellectuals, and journalists addressed these various audiences in their novels, essays, and articles, airing internal debates before a wider audience while offering their own positions and solutions. On the one hand, some claimed that Norwegians would inevitably merge with other groups, creating a unique American culture, and could therefore never hope to create an independent culture, although they might maintain a reverence for their Norwegian and Norwegian-American pasts. On the other hand, some argued that assimilation had too many costs, both for the Norwegians who would suffer a profound "spiritualessness" and for the Americans who could benefit from a flourishing Norwegian-American subculture.

In the context of an exacerbated and often hysterical nativism during World War I and its attendant Red Scare, these debates became heated and infused with a more powerful immediacy than they had been before. Nativistic attacks on Norwegian Americans led to a larger deliberation on anti-hyphenism in general within the ethnic community. Were "hyphenated" Americans disloyal, ignoring the reasonable call for 100% Americanism? Or did the cultivation of ethnic values enhance and enrich American culture? These were the parameters of the abstract debate that, after U.S. entry into the war, became a more concrete discussion over language-use, politics, and ethnic activities. In the context of this confusion, the end of the war mattered little both in terms of the national nativist movement, which continued well into the 1920s, and in terms of the ongoing controversies and debates within the Norwegian-American community itself. The general response of the community to wartime nativism was a resurgence of ethnic activity, including the enormous success of a Norwegian-American literature that confronted issues of ethnicity, Americanization, and nativism. The revitalization and creation of ethnic organizations and historical societies could be viewed as a reaction to nativism and the growing restrictionist movement. Threats from within and without the Norwegian-American community were ubiquitous. The loyalist Hazel Knapps and the children hiding in the cornfield to speak Norwegian made real historical choices in times of real historical struggles. The issues emanating from these struggles became encoded and ritualized in the Centennial celebration.

Cultural critics have demonstrated that we construct narratives about our history and our world that are rooted in myths and stories that reinforce a particular view of that world.[2] Historians who have recently begun to study celebrations and public events demonstrate the importance of history and the use of traditions in the creation of these events. Michael Frisch, for example, notes "the centrality of the relationship between history and the process of memory," individual and collective. "What matters," he continues, "is not so much the history placed before us, but rather what we are able to remember, and what role that knowledge plays in our lives."[3] George Lipsitz has recently argued that competing historical narratives in popular culture "are not just fights about the past, [but] they also transform cultural identity and political dialogue in the present." The values constructed in these narratives "are struggled over and contested every day on innumerable fronts and in countless arenas."[4] Indeed, as historian Jan Assmann points out, the "human" interest in the past has not been "any general 'historical' interest, but [has been] guided by other motives: namely a specific interest in legitimation, justification, reconciliation and change." In light of this, Assmann compellingly argues, "it is possible to inquire into the 'incentives' . . . and 'quietives' . . . of historical memory—i.e., its triggering and impeding factors." In other words, our motives for both remembering and forgetting are crucial.[5] As Lipsitz puts it, "What we choose to remember about the past, where we begin and end our retrospective accounts, and who we include and exclude from them—these do a lot to determine how we live and what decisions we make in the present."[6]

This sense of history and memory is crucial for any analysis of the invention of ethnicity. For ethnic self-representation is inextricably tied to a sense of the past. Until very recently, historians have understood that past as static traditions and values. That past, however, is dynamic, dependent on the needs and desires of the present. The Norwegian-American Centennial organizers in 1925, for example, created a past that served to legitimate their present positions as middle-class professionals in an ethnic community that was not a threat to American values and ideals. That very use of the past, however, was based on a powerful sense of Norwegian "uniqueness," which was indeed a threat to the dominant American ideal of homogeneity and conformity.

The Centennial's middle-class organizers also made real historical choices at "a moment of danger." They constructed their own historical narrative through specific representations of Norwegian-American history that signified their ethnicity as "safe" for American politics, business, and culture. In creating such a vision, the organizers sought to unite disparate members of the community under a "symbolic umbrella" that claimed power and status for the Norwegian-American community and simultaneously defused the hostility of the larger culture by demonstrating that Norwegian-American values and ideals were perfectly compatible with those of American culture. In creating this identity, the organizers confronted two different threats to their positions as leaders in a viable ethnic community in the 1920s—threats from a supposedly homogenizing consumer culture that was drawing away their young people and from a larger culture that was increasingly hostile to differences of any kind.

Like the many World's Fairs and expositions beginning in the late nineteenth century, the Centennial was a celebration of progress and a lesson in cultural uplift that served some very narrow class interests. Underpinning the narrative were stories of two Norwegian migrations to the New World: the pagan Vikings and the pioneers of 1825. Such stories are a crucial source of cultural legitimation, and not uncommon among ethnic groups. In their famous Yankee City series, anthropologist W. Lloyd Warner and his colleagues chronicled such a process in the founder's day celebration sponsored by the city elite.[7] Assmann argues that when historical time is "internalized," it becomes mythical time, or "a time of becoming." The past is not simply a remote event, but is organized in narrative form and serves an ongoing function: "either it becomes the 'engine of development,' to use Lévi-Strauss's term, or it furnishes the basis for continuity." As Assmann states, "myth is past that has been condensed into founding story."[8] The Norwegian-American founding story[ies] was meant both as an "engine of development" and a "basis for continuity." The organizers wanted to continue as leaders of a strong ethnic community that could go on to develop materially within an accepting American context. Not only did these stories parallel the dominant progressive narrative of expansion and linearity, but they also laid claim to a powerful Norwegian influence on western culture from at least A.D. 1000, the year of Leif Ericson's purported discovery of the New World. According to the organizers' narrative, the Vikings left a legacy of adventurousness and democracy that became part of not only Norwegian culture but also the cultures that they had conquered in western Europe. Add to that the pioneers' legacy of lawfulness and religious spirituality, and the resulting image suggests that Norwegian Americans were more American than the Yankees.

While there is evidence of this narrative strategy in the organization, structure, and content of the celebration, it is also evident in the stories the organizers chose not to tell. They told mythic stories of Vikings and pioneers whose innately democratic nature helped to found modern American culture. They did not tell stories about the many Norwegian-American men and women involved in attempts to radically transform American society through class and gender politics, ethnics who also invoked a Norwegian history and past to legitimate their activities. Through both their inclusions and exclusions, organizers created a seamless web that masked the long history of debates and dissension among Norwegian Americans about politics and ethnicity. For their efforts at presenting a nonpolitical ethnicity with explicit ties to the business community, President Coolidge, in his speech, called for a new selective immigration policy so that the United States could allow more Norwegians into the country.

The organizers' construction of Norwegian-American ethnicity points to an important though greatly under-studied aspect of ethnicity—the tension between the community as an entity voluntarily united by shared histories and values and the community as an economic unit pooling resources for mutual gain. Some historians have demonstrated how "moral values" sometimes superseded "economic" values,[9] but few scholars have been willing to explore the ways in which moral values like ethnic solidarity may in fact have been coercive economic strategies designed to claim resources that would have been otherwise unavailable. Thus, for example, when Rolvaag finds Norwegian Americans acting like American capitalists, he claims that they are undermining important "folk values." He does not see, however, that a significant part of the celebration of these folk values at the Centennial was a class strategy designed to compel conformity at one stage of the community's economic development. At the same time that the organizers made explicit connections to the local business community while suppressing Norwegian-American connections to labor politics, they presented a heroic Viking and pioneer past that signified a Norwegian Americanism that paralleled American ideals of expansion, individuality, and linearity.

Such a construction was not unusual. In the larger context of public memory, as Bodnar points out, after World War I and the attendant increase in federal power and nationalism, "ethnic memory became acceptable only if the public or patriotic stood above the personal and vernacular dimensions of the pioneer or the homeland symbols." Vernacular culture itself came to serve political and commercial interests. Bodnar posits the Centennial as an example of this changing nature of ethnic memory, emphasizing the powerful patriotic rhetoric.[10] This political process was complicated, however, by the alternative visions offered to participants who may have viewed the world in very different and contradictory ways.

The organizers' narrative was, as we have seen, highly unstable, equivocal, and contradictory. On the one hand, the symbolic objects and civic rituals helped to suspend internal conflict among the participants in favor of a very particular and controlled vision of ethnicity. However, the ambiguity and polyvalence of those very same rituals and symbols speak to a more complex and contested construction of Norwegian-American ethnicity. The organizers' use of the past turned back on itself in ways that made their narrative quite unstable. They invoked a mythic Viking and pioneer past as compatible with American ideals; however, they presented this vision in terms of ethnicity, which was itself a threat to the dominant assimilationist ideology. Furthermore, because of their Viking past, Norwegian Americans were not simply eligible to be good Americans, they were better Americans than so-called Yankees. Such a notion inverted the nativist narrative without questioning its premises. While such a strategy was self-defeating in many important ways, it relied on a historical memory of Norwegian romantic nationalism that created room for alternative visions of ethnicity, which in turn subverted the organizers' efforts.

In these terms, the Centennial was a celebration not of American progress, but of Norwegian-American progress. Norway, not America, was the redemptive sacred space in both the organizers' vision and the alternative narratives present at the Centennial in Rolvaag's speech, Ager's essay, and the exhibits of memorabilia and heirlooms. Though nationalism was invoked by Norwegian Americans for some often contradictory reasons, it nonetheless signified that Norwegian Americans were a "peculiar" people—a strategy that inverted and challenged the dominant "melting pot" ideal. Furthermore, scholars of romantic nationalism have demonstrated that nationalism's categories appeal to emotion and desire, to a sense of connectedness and simultaneity with an "imagined community." This "naturalized" community functions within a powerful language of kinship, familiarity, and circularity.[11] As demonstrated repeatedly throughout the celebration and in its culminating pageant, immigrant contributions to America depended upon "uniquely" Norwegian characteristics. While these characteristics, according to the organizers, were not a threat to a unified American culture, their dependence upon a Norwegian nationalism was. Norwegian nationalism competed with Americanism throughout the celebration, making much more contradictory the apparently seamless narrative of the organizers.

Though nationalism refers to a nation-state, a homeland, the language of nationalism is an important part of the invention of ethnic identities in a multicultural society. The language of nationalism depends on an idealized past, on a desire for symbolic order. Such a need in an industrialized society is part of the nineteenth-century "invention of tradition" described by Eric Hobsbawm.[12] That desire is perhaps one reason that ethnicity became such an important signifier of identity. Like the family, it was presumed to be a stable referent outside of history—not because it was, but because capitalism's revolutionary project of fragmentation created a need for a constructed stable referent. The danger, of course, is that that "stable" referent continually promises possibility and feeds desire, creating room for a world where ethnic memory opposed dominant American values of conformity, individualism, and inevitable progress. In the hands of Rolvaag, for example, nationalist language could form a biting critique of American culture—and Americanizing Norwegians. Such a world is always available for negotiation or opposition.

The year 1925 was significant in Norwegian-American history. According to historians of the Norwegian-American experience and the criteria set by a generation of immigration historians, the community was rapidly assimilating and Americanizing. Norwegian language-use was on the wane, ethnic institutions were no longer the center of community life, and many people were benefiting from the new consumerism, moving rapidly into middle-class life and out of the ethnic neighborhoods. The Centennial, with its profusion of Americanist rhetoric, was merely a nostalgic look at the past. Celebrations, however, are important sites for the construction of meaning and "a look at the past" is a crucial component of that construction. The Centennial celebration teaches us that to be "ethnic" is not to subscribe to a "primordial," natural set of values and beliefs. Rather, to be "ethnic" is to engage in a dynamic process of self-definition, of creativity and invention, that may have very little to do with any "authentic" and stable Old World culture. Both the cultural content of ethnicity and its use are grounded in specific historical contexts and change over time. Such a concept of invention allows instead of assimilation a dynamic model of both accommodation and resistance.

Indeed, some institutions were in fact revitalized for a time after the Centennial. Several new *lags* were organized either at the celebration or after; a film of the Centennial made the rounds of local communities and lodges in an attempt to maintain the momentum and euphoria of the celebration itself; and the Norse-American Centennial Daughters were active throughout the 1920s and 1930s in promoting Norwegian culture in general and such things as a Leif Ericson memorial in particular. May 17 celebrations, more "Norway Days," and a sesquicentennial in 1975 (held in several cities and communities) continued the celebratory aspects of Norwegian-American ethnicity. In some important ways, however, it could be argued that the Norwegian-American historians are correct. In terms of the traditional categories of immigration history—institutions, language-use, neighborhoods—Norwegian-American ethnicity was not the same after the 1920s. Nor was it the same before the 1920s. If we think of ethnicity as an ongoing process of identity-formation, however, such categories beg the question. The Centennial was not merely a "final rally" of ethnic forces, as we have seen, but a tension-filled and ambivalent effort at cultural legitimation at a particular historical moment.

One immediate and long-lasting result of the Centennial was the organization of the Norwegian-American Historical Association. The Centennial celebration served as the final impetus for planning and organizing the Association. Echoing the Centennial rhetoric, D. G. Ristad wrote in the first issue of the Association's journal, "While adjusting themselves to the new environment, [Norwegian Americans] have taken seriously their responsibility in the forming of the type of American racial individuality which is being produced out of composite elements; conscious of their backgrounds and origins, they have desired to give to the new nation the best elements in their nature and their cultural experience. Thus they have recognized an obligation both to the past and to posterity." Like other hereditary societies organized in the 1920s, the Association wanted to "collect and preserve records and objects that throw light upon the activities" of Norwegian Americans, and it wanted to promote and publish historical research.[13] Out of the Association's press grew a body of historical monographs that chronicled the contributions of Norwegians to American society and their steady, inexorable transition from a static "folk" culture to a melding with a unified American culture. Many of these monographs end with the Centennial, a last nostalgic look backward.[14]

However, at the same time that he was involved in the Centennial and in organizing the Association, Rolvaag wrote his prize-winning *Giants in the Earth*, the most popular Norwegian-American novel and a harsh critique of American culture and the immigration process. The same scholars who write Norwegian-American history as the immigrant success story also revere Rolvaag as a "patron saint" of Norwegian-American culture. A colleague once told me that at one of the many conferences on Rolvaag held at St. Olaf College in recent years, the chair ended the conference by leading the conferees to Rolvaag's grave, where they remembered the author. The historian noted this "bizarre" experience as emblematic of this particular community's reverence for Rolvaag.

These contradictory aspects of Norwegian-American ethnicity continue to play an important role in Norwegian Americans' self-representation and historical memory. In July of each year, Norwegian Americans and others gather in Minnehaha Park in Minneapolis to celebrate Norway Day. Organized by lodges and local businesses, the celebration is reminiscent of the 1925 Centennial in content if not in scale. People gather in the park to renew old acquaintances, listen to speeches, hear Norwegian folk music, and watch Norwegian folk dancers.

At the July 1990, celebration, participants worshipped in Norwegian and English, listened to speeches about Norwegian contributions to America and the Norwegian heritage, watched a parade of notable Norwegian Americans introduced, and sang both the American and Norwegian national anthems. Norwegian and American flags festooned the souvenir program as well as the stage. In addition to advertisements congratulating Norwegian Americans on their fine heritage and inviting them on tours of Norway, the souvenir program also included an essay on the American Constitution. Such conservative elements are reminiscent of the Centennial celebration and the organizers' middle-class narrative. The Norwegian heritage is important for the contributions it has made to world culture, but notably, it is completely compatible with American ideals and values.

Participants were also treated to a performance by the recently organized Viking Age Club, whose traveling living-history exhibit was devoted to rewriting Viking history to exclude the more violent aspects of conquest. At the same time, participants could also watch young children and teenagers dressed in Norwegian national peasant costumes dance and parade throughout the park. The costumes for both the Vikings and the children could have been worn for the 1925 pageant. Unlike the Centennial, however, participants could purchase "Norwegian" memorabilia and crafts: troll dolls, rosemaling, woodwork, and jewelry made of silverware imported from Norway.

The only performing group from Norway, young men and women calling themselves "The Oldtimers," played and danced to Norwegian folk music. They were not dressed like all of the Norwegian-American performers in national costumes, however; they wore neon shorts and T-shirts, and sported "new age" haircuts. This group starkly, indeed humorously, pointed to the contrast between contemporary Norwegian culture and the idealized past that signified a Norwegian-American identity for many at this celebration. In this context, such an identity appears quaint and nostalgic, something to be commodified and consumed every third Sunday in July. Like the Centennial, however, such a cultural creation speaks to its audience in open-ended and contradictory ways. This construction of Norwegian-American ethnicity holds such power that, according to one story I've heard, students from St. Olaf College on Norway exchanges have an unusually difficult time adjusting to contemporary Norwegian culture, a culture that bears little resemblance to their *idea* of what it means to be Norwegian. Whether this is true or not, the story itself speaks to the problematic ways in which contemporary ethnic Americans idealize their immigrant pasts.

One could argue that the ethnicity evident at Norway Day and at the Centennial was merely a "symbolic ethnicity," that is, an ethnicity that has little effect on everyday life. It is chosen as a leisure-time activity—a St. Patrick's Day parade, a traditional family holiday. But it is not supported by a collective, institutional community.[15] To say that such an ethnicity is "merely" symbolic, however, is to misunderstand the powerfully ideological place of ethnicity in American life. In her recent study of white middle-class ethnicity, for example, Mary C. Waters demonstrates that "choosing" ethnic identification, even in as tenuous a form as a pair of Austrian mountain pants or Italian food on Christmas, is historically variable and has ramifications for the way we think about the world. On one level, Waters argues, such identification speaks to a desire for community, though a community without "individual cost." On a more pernicious level, such "symbolic ethnicity" among the white middle class reinforces racism by masking the powerful inequalities in ethnic heritages. Indeed, many of her informants implied that their Irish or Italian ancestors suffered discrimination but "made it" without the need for affirmative action. In such an ideology, blacks, Asians, and Hispanics should be proud of their heritages, but not "use" them to gain advantage.[16]

The conservative, accommodationist ethnicity at the Centennial in 1925 and at Norway Day in 1990 certainly supports Waters's hypothesis. There are moments, however, when that conservatism is contested. Like the Centennial, Norway Day also serves as a time for lodge and *bygdelag* reunions. This sense of community and renewal was clearly important to many participants; it was the reason to attend. While this is a sense of community without daily constraints, it nonetheless speaks to a larger desire for belonging—a physical and historical belonging. Furthermore, the overt construction of Norwegian-American history at the celebration was not unproblematic. I spoke to one woman who opposed the whole premise of the Viking Age Club, arguing that Norwegian Americans should neither "cover up" that part of their history nor glorify it. She noted that more recent Norwegian history—a welfare state that takes care of its people—is perhaps more "useful" to remember.

If we think of ethnicity as a static set of values that is passed on from generation to generation, values that become trivialized and commodified as a group achieves middle-class status, we miss the continually negotiated and contingent nature of ethnic identities. To say that ethnicity is an invention, furthermore, is not to say that there is a "free marketplace" of identities available for the taking. The invention of ethnicity—what we choose to remember and what we choose to forget—is grounded in social experience and the politics of culture.

Notes
✛

Prologue

1. "15,000 See Pageant, Bring Norse Celebration to Close," *St. Paul Pioneer Press*, 10 June 1925, 1.
2. See David Glassberg, *American Historical Pageantry: The Uses of Tradition in the Early Twentieth Century* (Chapel Hill: University of North Carolina Press, 1990).
3. The following descriptions of the pageant performance are taken from "Directions for Producing the 'Pageant of the Northmen'" and "Pageant of the Northmen," by Willard Dillman, Norse-American Centennial Papers, Box 4, Norwegian-American Historical Association, Northfield, Minnesota.
4. Dillman, "Pageant of the Northmen," 1.
5. Karen Larsen, *A History of Norway* (Princeton: Princeton University Press, 1948); T. K. Derry, *A History of Modern Norway, 1814–1972* (Oxford: Clarendon Press, 1973).
6. Peter A. Munch, "Norwegians," in *Harvard Encyclopedia of American Ethnic Groups*, ed. Stephan Thernstrom et al. (Cambridge: Belknap Press of Harvard University Press, 1980), 250–51; Carleton C. Qualey and Jon A. Gjerde, "The Norwegians," in *They Chose Minnesota: A Survey of the State's Ethnic Groups*, ed. June Drenning Holmquist (St. Paul: Minnesota Historical Society, 1981), 220–21; Theodore Blegen, *Norwegian Migration to America: The American Transition* (Northfield, Minn.: Norwegian-American Historical Association, 1940); Ingrid Semmingsen, *Norway to America: A History of Migration*, trans. Einar Haugen (Minneapolis: University of Minnesota Press, 1978).
7. Dillman, "Directions for Producing 'Pageant of the Northmen,'" 8.
8. Ibid., 9–10.
9. "Pageant of the Northmen," 17.
10. Ibid., 18–21.
11. Ibid., 24.

1. Ethnic Identity and Celebration

1. O. M. Norlie, "Why We Celebrate," *Norse-American Centennial, 1825–1925: Souvenir Edition* (Minneapolis, 1925), 55–56.
2. Quoted in Carl Chrislock, *Ethnicity Challenged: The Upper Midwest Norwegian American Experience in WWI* (Northfield, Minn.: Norwegian-American Historical Association, 1981), 38.
3. Odd Sverre Lovoll, *The Promise of America: A History of the Norwegian-American People* (Minneapolis: University of Minnesota, 1984), 195–96. I will discuss and note these historians of the Norwegian-American experience in more detail later in this chapter.

4. Recent works dealing with issues of cultural inventions of tradition include *The Invention of Tradition,* ed. Eric Hobsbawm and Terence Ranger (Cambridge: Cambridge University Press, 1985). Rudolph Vecoli has applied Hobsbawm's ideas to ethnic communities in " 'Primo Maggio' in the U.S.: An Invented Tradition of the Italian Anarchists," in *May Day Celebration,* ed. Andrea Panaccione, Quaderni della Fondazione G. Brodolini (Veneci: Marsilio Editori, 1988), 55–83. John Bodnar also applies Hobsbawm in "Symbols and Servants: Immigrant America and the Limits of Public History," *Journal of American History* 73 (June 1986): 137–51. See also Bodnar, *Remaking America: Public Memory, Commemoration, and Patriotism in the Twentieth Century* (Princeton: Princeton University Press, 1992). Recent scholars in cultural studies have also worked innovatively with ideas of creativity and cultural invention. See in particular Michael Fischer, "Ethnicity and the Post-Modern Arts of Memory," in *Writing Culture,* ed. James Clifford and George Marcus (Berkeley: University of California Press, 1985), 194–233; Ramon Gutierrez, *When Jesus Came, The Corn Mothers Went Away: Marriage, Sexuality and Power in New Mexico, 1500–1846* (Palo Alto: Stanford University Press, 1990); George Lipsitz, "Mardi Gras Indians: Carnival and Counter-Narrative in Black New Orleans," *Cultural Critique* 10 (Fall 1988): 99–122; Karen Isaksen Leonard, *Making Ethnic Choices: California's Punjabi Mexican Americans* (Philadelphia: Temple University Press, 1992); Werner Sollors, *Beyond Ethnicity: Consent and Descent in American Culture* (New York: Oxford University Press, 1986); and Sollors, ed., *The Invention of Ethnicity* (New York: Oxford University Press, 1989).

5. Nancy Fraser, "Rethinking the Public Sphere: A Contribution to the Critique of Actually Existing Democracy," in *Habermas and the Public Sphere,* ed. Craig Calhoun (Cambridge: MIT Press, 1992), 123.

6. Certainly not all Norwegian Americans were middle class. Jon Gjerde, however, has demonstrated that Norwegians, particularly in the upper Midwest, moved steadily toward middle-class status, if not in actuality at least in desire. And the narrative created by the Centennial organizers was middle class. See Jon Gjerde, *From Peasants to Farmers: The Migration from Balestrand, Norway, to the Upper Midwest* (Cambridge: Cambridge University Press, 1985).

7. Elizabeth Ewen, *Immigrant Women in the Land of Dollars: Life and Culture on the Lower East Side, 1890–1925* (New York: Monthly Review Press, 1985), 13.

8. The classical assimilationist works in history and sociology include Oscar Handlin, *The Uprooted* (Boston: Little, Brown, 1951); William I. Thomas and Florian Znaniecki, *The Polish Peasant in Europe and America* (Boston: Knopf, 1927); Robert Park, *Race and Culture* (Glencoe, Ill.: Free Press, 1950); and Milton Gordon, *Assimilation in American Life* (New York: Oxford University Press, 1964). Stephan Thernstrom, *Poverty and Progress: Social Mobility in a Nineteenth-Century City* (Cambridge: Harvard University Press, 1964), was the classic mobility study that built upon the assimilationist model.

9. John Bodnar, *The Transplanted: A History of Immigrants in Urban America* (Bloomington: Indiana University Press, 1985), 205.

10. Virginia Yans-McLaughlin, ed., *Immigration Reconsidered: History, Sociology, and Politics* (New York: Oxford University Press, 1990).

11. Bodnar's synthesis built upon the work of 1970s scholars who established theories of a cross-continental capitalist system of migration that greatly influenced both the numbers and the kinds of people who emigrated. See especially Josef Barton, *Peasants and Strangers: Italians, Rumanians, and Slovaks in an American City, 1890–1950* (Cambridge: Harvard University Press, 1975).

12. Olivier Zunz, "American History and the Changing Meaning of Assimilation," *Journal of American Ethnic History* 4 (Spring 1985): 55, 57, 63. For other critiques of both the classical assimilationist studies and the new pluralistic approaches to immigration and ethnicity, see Harold Abramson, "Assimilation and Pluralism Theories," in *Harvard Encyclopedia of American Ethnic Groups*, 150–60; Nathan Glazer and Daniel P. Moynihan, eds., *Ethnicity: Theory and Experience* (Cambridge: MIT Press, 1978); and John Higham, "Current Trends in the Study of Ethnicity in the United States," *Journal of American Ethnic History* 1 (1982): 5–16.

13. John Higham, *Send These to Me: Jews and Other Immigrants in Urban America* (Baltimore: Johns Hopkins University Press, 1984), 242, 232.

14. Bodnar, *The Transplanted*, 205.

15. Yans-McLaughlin, *Immigration Reconsidered*.

16. Carl Chrislock, "The First Two Centennials: 1914 and 1925," *Norwegian-American Sesquicentennial, 1825–1975* (Minneapolis, 1975): 34.

17. Chrislock, *Ethnicity Challenged*, 15, 48, 139.

18. Lovoll, *The Promise of America*, 195–96.

19. When I refer to a body of historical work on the Norwegian Americans, I am referring to works published from 1925 to the present. These major works include: O. M. Norlie, *A History of the Norwegian People in America* (Minneapolis, 1925); Carlton Qualey, *Norwegian Settlement in the United States* (Northfield, Minn.: Norwegian-American Historical Association, 1938); Blegen, *Norwegian Migration to America*; Einar Haugen, *The Norwegian Language in America: A Study in Bilingual Behavior* (Bloomington: Indiana University Press, 1969); Jon Wefald, *A Voice of Protest: Norwegians in American Politics, 1890–1917* (Northfield, Minn.: Norwegian-American Historical Association, 1971); Arlow Anderson, *The Norwegian Americans* (Boston: Twayne, 1975); Odd Lovoll, *A Folk Epic: The 'Bygedlag' in America* (Boston: Twayne Publishers, 1975); Odd Lovoll, ed., *Cultural Pluralism versus Assimilation: The Views of Waldemar Ager* (Northfield, Minn.: Norwegian American Historical Association, 1977); Semmingsen, *Norway to America*; Chrislock, *Ethnicity Challenged*; Lovoll, *The Promise of America*; Jon Gjerde, *From Peasants to Farmers*; Odd Lovoll, *A Century of Urban Life: Norwegians in Chicago before 1930* (Northfield, Minn.: Norwegian-American Historical Association, 1988).

20. Blegen, *Norwegian Migration to America*, 99, 81.

21. Lovoll, *The Promise of America*, ix.

22. See Fredrick Barth, *Ethnic Groups and Boundaries* (Boston: Little, Brown, 1970).

23. Patricia Albers and William R. James, "On the Dialectics of Ethnicity: To Be or Not to Be Santee (Sioux)," *Journal of Ethnic Studies* 14 (Spring 1986): 10.

24. Orlando Patterson, *Ethnic Chauvinism: The Reactionary Impulse* (New York: Stein and Day, 1977).

25. E. L. Cerroni-Long, "Ideology and Ethnicity: An American-Soviet Comparison," *Journal of Ethnic Studies* 14 (Fall 1986): 20.

26. Sollors, *The Invention of Ethnicity,* x, xi. Sollors has made a similar argument in *Beyond Ethnicity.*

27. Renato Resaldo, "Others of Invention: Ethnicity and Its Discontents," *Village Voice Literary Supplement,* 82 (Feb. 1990): 27.

28. Fischer, "Ethnicity and the Post-Modern Arts of Memory," 20.

29. For discussions of hegemony in these terms see, Stuart Hall, "Gramsci's Relevance for the Study of Race and Ethnicity," *Journal of Communication Inquiry* 10 (Summer 1986): 20–21; and George Lipsitz, "The Struggle for Hegemony," *Journal of American History* 75 (June 1988): 146–51.

30. In *Emigrants and Exiles: Ireland and the Irish Exodus to North America* (New York: Oxford University Press, 1985), Kerby Miller convincingly demonstrates the construction of a middle-class Irish-American ethnicity that was very similar to the middle-class narrative created by the organizers of the Norwegian-American Centennial. Miller, however, argues that the Irish working class who defined themselves as ethnic accepted the hegemony of this middle-class ethnicity, leaving no room for alternative definitions or interpretations of what it means to be Irish in America.

31. John Kirkpatrick, "Trials of Identity in America," *Cultural Anthropology* 4 (August 1989): 303.

32. Robert Orsi is one of the few historians to take celebration within an ethnic community as the primary site of analysis for a book-length study. See Robert Orsi, *The Madonna of 115th Street: Faith and Community in Italian Harlem, 1880–1950* (New Haven: Yale University Press, 1985). See also Kathleen Neils Conzen, "Ethnicity as Festive Culture: Nineteenth-Century German America on Parade," in Sollors, *The Invention of Ethnicity,* 44–76; and Bodnar, *Remaking America,* passim.

33. See Allesandro Falassi, ed., *Time Out of Time: Essays on the Festival* (Albuquerque: University of New Mexico Press, 1987); Don Handelman, *Models and Mirrors: Towards an Anthropology of Public Events* (Cambridge: Cambridge University Press, 1990); John MacAloon, ed., *Rite, Drama, Festival, Spectacle: Rehearsals Toward a Theory of Cultural Performance* (Philadelphia: Institute for the Study of Human Issues, 1984); Sally Falk Moore and Barbara Myerhoff, eds., *Symbol and Politics in Communal Ideology* (Ithaca: Cornell University Press, 1975); Victor Turner, ed., *Celebrations: Studies in Festivity and Ritual* (Washington, D.C.: Smithsonian Institution Press, 1982).

34. Susan G. Davis, *Parades and Power: Street Theatre in Nineteenth-Century Philadelphia* (Philadelphia: Temple University Press, 1986).

35. Bodnar, *Remaking America,* 14.

2. *"To Lose the Unspeakable"*

1. See especially Blegen, *Norwegian Migration to America;* Anderson, *The Norwegian Americans;* and Lovoll, *The Promise of America.*

2. Tzvetan Todorov, *The Conquest of America: The Question of the Other* (New York: Harper and Row, 1984), 247.

3. Horace Kallen, *Culture and Democracy in the United States* (New York: Boni and Liveright, 1924), 43. This volume is a compilation of Kallen's essays written from 1914 to 1924.

4. John Higham, *Strangers in the Land: Patterns of American Nativism, 1860–1925* (New Brunswick, N.J.: Rutgers University Press, 1988), 23, 25.

5. Quoted in ibid., 30.

6. E. A. Ross, *The Old World in the New* (New York: Century, 1914), 287.

7. See Higham, *Strangers in the Land;* Henry Fairchild, "The Restriction of Immigration," *American Journal of Sociology* 17 (March 1912): 637–46; Alvin Kogut, "The Settlements and Ethnicity: 1890–1914," *Social Work* 17 (1971): 22–31; Edward Hartmann, *The Movement to Americanize the Immigrant* (Baltimore: Johns Hopkins University Press, 1948); and Gerd Korman, *Industrialism, Immigrants and Americanizers* (Madison: University of Wisconsin Press, 1967).

8. Bodnar, *Remaking America,* 21.

9. Carl Chrislock, *Watchdog of Loyalty: The Minnesota Commission of Public Safety During World War I* (St. Paul: Minnesota Historical Society Press, 1991), 20.

10. See Frederick Luebke, *The Bonds of Loyalty: German Americans and World War I* (De Kalb: Northern Illinois University Press, 1974).

11. See Bodnar, *The Transplanted,* 144–86, for a discussion of the dissension in immigrant churches, particularly in urban America.

12. Dorothy Skardahl, *The Divided Heart: Scandinavian Immigrant Experience Through Literary Sources* (Lincoln: University of Nebraska Press, 1974), 181.

13. Duane Rodell Lindberg, *Men of the Cloth and the Social-Cultural Fabric of the Norwegian Ethnic Community in North Dakota* (New York: Arno Press, 1980), 277.

14. Chrislock, "Introduction," in Lovoll, *Cultural Pluralism versus Assimilation,* 17.

15. See ibid., and Lovoll, *The Promise of America.*

16. Lovoll, *A Folk Epic.*

17. Ibid., 148. Lovoll is quoting Olav Redal, *Decorah-Posten,* 22 July 1927.

18. Chrislock, *Ethnicity Challenged,* 21.

19. Ibid., 22.

20. Johs. B. Wist, "Our Cultural Stage," *Kvartalskrift* 1 (January 1905), trans. Lovoll, *Cultural Pluralism versus Assimilation,* 39.

21. Waldemar Ager, "Our Cultural Possibilities," *Kvartalskrift* 2 (April 1905), trans., in Lovoll, *Cultural Pluralism versus Assimilation,* 47.

22. See Einar Haugen, *Immigrant Idealist: A Literary Biography of Waldemar Ager, Norwegian American* (Northfield, Minn.: Norwegian-American Historical Association, 1989); Clarence Kilde, "Tragedy in the Life and Writings of Waldemar Ager:

Norwegian Immigrant, Author, and Editor, 1869–1941" (MA Thesis, University of Minnesota, 1978).

23. Waldemar Ager, "Preserving Our Mother Tongue," *Kvartalskrift* 14 (October 1905), trans., in Lovoll, *Cultural Pluralism versus Assimilation*, 55, 57.

24. O. E. Rolvaag, *"Amerika-Breve," American Prefaces* 1 (April 1936), 110–2. In her personal notes on the Jorgenson and Solum biography of Rolvaag (*Ole Edvart Rolvaag: A Biography* [New York: Harper and Brothers, 1939]), Jennie Rolvaag noted that her husband delivered this passage as a speech in 1903. Jennie Rolvaag's Notes on the Jorgenson and Solum Biography, Box 41, Rolvaag Papers, Norwegian-American Historical Association, Northfield, Minnesota.

25. Rolvaag, *"Amerika-Breve"*, 110.

26. Haugen, *Norwegian Language in America*, 253.

27. Ibid., 233, 234.

28. Rolvaag to Percy Boynton, Box 41, Rolvaag Papers.

29. Rolvaag, *Peder Victorious* (Lincoln: University of Nebraska Press, 1982), 177.

30. See ibid.; Blegen, *Norwegian Migration to America;* Lovoll, *The Promise of America;* E. Clifford Nelson, *The Lutheran Church among Norwegian Americans* (Minneapolis: Augsburg Publishing House, 1960).

31. Lindberg, *Men of the Cloth*, 20, 132.

32. Haugen, *Norwegian Language in America*, 239.

33. Skardahl, *The Divided Heart*, 295.

34. My evidence about these texts, which were published in Norwegian, comes from Gerald Thorson, "Tinsel and Dust: Disenchantment in Two Minneapolis Novels from the 1880s," *Minnesota History* 45 (1977): 210–22.

35. Ibid., 222.

36. In this case, we can place the Jansons' novels in the same context with Theodore Dreiser's *Sister Carrie* (1900) and Upton Sinclair's *The Jungle* (1906), among others.

37. Quoted in Jorgensen and Solum, *Ole Edvart Rolvaag: A Biography* (New York: Harper and Brothers, 1939), 100.

38. Quoted in Lindberg, *Men of the Cloth*, 37.

3. *"The Day of the Great Beast"*

1. O. E. Rolvaag, *Pure Gold* (New York: Harper and Brothers, 1930), 229, 234. This is the first English translation of this novel. It was originally published in Norwegian as *To Tullinger* (Two Fools) in 1920.

2. From *Lutheranen*, 11 December 1918, as quoted in Einar Haugen, *Ole Edvart Rolvaag* (Boston: Twayne, 1983), 44.

3. Ibid., 237.

4. Ibid., 48.

5. Rolvaag Diary, Box 39, Rolvaag Papers.

6. Conversation with Betty Bergland, 17 July 1990. I would like to thank Bergland for her sensitive interpretation of this common immigrant situation.

7. Reprinted in Randolph Bourne, *The Radical Will: Selected Writings, 1911–1918* (New York: Urizen Books, 1977), 248.

8. Lovoll, *A Folk Epic*, 147.

9. Horace Kallen, *Culture and Democracy in the United States*, 12.

10. Leonard Dinnerstein, *The Leo Frank Case* (New York: Columbia University Press, 1968). This case points not only to anti-Semitism, but also to the process of "scapegoating" by southerners who were threatened more by the northern industrialist in Leo Frank than the Jew in an era of increasing industrial change in that region. As Dinnerstein points out, many southerners clung to the agrarian past, focusing on their Anglo-Saxon heritage to an often violently xenophobic degree.

11. Higham, *Strangers in the Land*, 186.

12. See Luebke, *Bonds of Loyalty*.

13. Higham, *Strangers in the Land*, 211, 262.

14. Ibid., 195–205.

15. Quoted in Chrislock, *Ethnicity Challenged*, 35.

16. Quoted in Wefald, *A Voice of Protest*, 73–74 (from *The Congressional Record*, 53:1700, 54:831 (appendix) and *Fram*, 29 March 1917), 75.

17. Chrislock, *Ethnicity Challenged*, 55. For a specific discussion of Norwegian Americans involved in radical politics, see Chapter four.

18. Chrislock, "Introduction," to Lovoll, *Cultural Pluralism*, 25.

19. Chrislock, *Ethnicity Challenged*, 39.

20. Chrislock, "Introduction," to Lovoll, *Cultural Pluralism*, 28.

21. Chrislock, *Ethnicity Challenged*, 40, 44.

22. Ibid., 39–40.

23. Lovoll, *A Folk Epic*, 147.

24. Chrislock, *Ethnicity Challenged*, 41.

25. Waldemar Ager, "The Melting Pot," *Kvartalskrift* 33 (April 1916), trans., in Lovoll, *Cultural Pluralism versus Assimilation*, 81, 86.

26. Chrislock, *Ethnicity Challenged*, 42, 43.

27. Quoted in Kilde, "Tragedy in the Life," 70.

28. Chrislock, *Ethnicity Challenged*, 56–57.

29. Ibid., 67.

30. Chrislock, *Watchdog of Loyalty*, 245.

31. Ibid., 70.

32. Ibid., 82.

33. Both quoted in Lovoll, *The Promise of America*, 193.

34. Quoted in Chrislock, *Ethnicity Challenged*, 84.

35. Lovoll, *Promise of America*, 114.

36. Bodnar, *The Transplanted*, 147.

37. Nelson, *The Lutheran Church Among Norwegian Americans*, 237.

38. Ibid., 241.

39. Quoted in Chrislock, *Ethnicity Challenged*, 84.

40. Haugen, *Norwegian Language in America*, 256, 257.

41. Rolvaag, "Reflections on Our Heritage," Unpublished manuscript translated by Brynhild Rowberg, 1982, Rolvaag Papers.

42. Bodnar, *Remaking America*, 41.

4. *"The Pride of the Race Had Been Touched"*

1. Quoted in Lovoll, *The Promise of America*, 195.

2. Mrs. John O. Lee, "The 'Living Flag,' " in *Souvenir: Norse-American Women, 1825–1925: A Symposium of Prose and Poetry, Newspaper Articles, and Biographies, Contributed by One Hundred Prominent Women*, ed. Alma A. Gutterson and Regina Hilleboe Christensen (Minneapolis: Lutheran Free Church Publishing Co., 1926), 122–23.

3. Alma A. Gutterson, "The Two Flags," in ibid., 184.

4. Norlie, "Why We Celebrate," 35, 55.

5. Eric Hobsbawm, "The Invention of Tradition," in Hobsbawm and Ranger, *The Invention of Tradition*, 1–14.

6. Kathleen Neils Conzen, David A. Gerber, Ewa Morawska, George Pozzetta, Rudy Vecoli, "The Invention of Ethnicity: A Perspective from the U.S.A.," *Altreitalie* (April 1990): 38–39. Print offset of a paper presented at the International Commission on Historical Demography, Madrid, August 1990.

7. Bodnar, *Remaking America*, 13.

8. Lovoll, *A Folk Epic*, 150–51.

9. N. T. Moen to S. H. Holstad, 4 August 1924, Box 1, Norse-American Centennial Papers (Archives of the Norwegian-American Historical Association, St. Olaf College, Northfield, Minnesota).

10. Judith Jacobs to Oscar Arneson, 25 April 1925, Box 2, Norse-American Centennial Papers.

11. David Glassberg, "Restoring a 'Forgotten Childhood': American Play and the Progressive Era's Elizabethan Past," *American Quarterly* 32 (Fall 1980): 359–62.

12. Glassberg, "History and the Public: Legacies of the Progressive Era," *Journal of American History* 73 (March 1987): 958, 959, 961. Glassberg bases his concept of the secular jeremiad on Sacvan Bercovitch, *The American Jeremiad* (Madison: University of Wisconsin Press, 1978).

13. Oscar Olson, Meeting Address, Decorah, Iowa, typescript, 12 November 1924, Box 3, Norse-American Centennial Papers.

14. For such arguments about the 1920s, see Paul Carter, *The Twenties in America* (London: Routledge and Kegan Paul, 1975); Richard Wightman Fox and T. J. Jackson Lears, eds., *The Culture of Consumption* (New York, 1983); Lary May, *Screening Out the Past: The Birth of Mass Culture and the Motion Picture Industry* (Chicago:

University of Chicago Press, 1983); and Helen M. Lynd and Robert S. Lynd, *Middletown: A Study in American Culture* (New York: Harcourt, Brace and World, 1929).

15. John R. Jenswold, "Becoming American, Becoming Suburban: Norwegians in the 1920s," *Norwegian-American Studies* 33 (1992): 5–6.

16. Lizbeth Cohen, "Encountering Mass Culture at the Grassroots: The Experience of Chicago Workers in the 1920s," *American Quarterly* 14 (March 1989): 6–33.

17. Jenswold, "Becoming American," 16–17.

18. O. E. Rolvaag, Lecture Notes, Box 20, File 39, Rolvaag Papers.

19. O. E. Rolvaag, "Reflections on Our Heritage," Unpublished Manuscript, Translated by Brynhild Rowberg, 1982, Rolvaag Papers.

20. Ragna Grimsby to Centennial Committee, 14 January 1925, Box 1, Norse-American Centennial Papers.

21. Jens Roseland to Centennial Committee, n.d., Box 1, Norse-American Centennial Papers.

22. See Higham, *Strangers in the Land.*

23. Sinclair Lewis, *Babbitt* (1922; New York: Signet Books, 1988), 150–5, 312.

24. S. H. Holstad to O. J. Kvale, 27 January 1925, Box 1, Norse-American Centennial Papers.

25. Knud Wefald to Gisle Bothne, 19 February 1925, Box 1, Gisle Bothne Papers, Minnesota Historical Society, St. Paul, Minnesota.

26. Quoted in Carl O. Pedersen, "The Norse-American Centennial" (1925), 84, Box 303, Carl O. Pedersen Papers, Norwegian-American Historical Society, Northfield, Minnesota.

27. Holstad to M. E. Waldeland, 15 April 1925, Box 3, Norse-American Centennial Papers.

28. O. M. Norlie, "Why We Celebrate," 53, 59.

29. E. G. Quamme to Gisle Bothne, September 1924, Box 1, Norse-American Centennial Papers.

30. Bulletin #7 from Centennial Committee to Local Organizers, 28 March 1925, Box 3, Norse-American Centennial Papers.

31. E. G. Quamme to County Ticket Sellers, 5 May 1925, Box 3, Norse-American Centennial Papers.

32. Broadcast Manuscript, 14 May 1925, Box 3, Norse-American Centennial Papers.

33. O. J. Kvale to S. H. Holstad, 29 January 1925, Box 3, Norse-American Centennial Papers.

34. Bulletin #7, 28 March 1925, Box 3, Norse-American Centennial Papers.

35. Quoted in Bulletin #5 from Centennial Committee to Local Organizers, March 9, 1925, Box 3, Norse-American Centennial Papers.

36. Frank E. Manning, "Cosmos and Chaos: Celebration in the Modern World," in *The Celebration of Society: Perspectives on Contemporary Cultural Performance,* ed. Frank E. Manning (Bowling Green: Bowling Green University Popular Press, 1983), 6–7.

37. Stuart Hall, "The Narrative Construction of Reality," *Southern Review* 17 (March 1984): 8, 11.

38. Raymond Williams, *Marxism and Literature* (Oxford: Oxford University Press, 1977), 108–27.

39. "Kellogg Warns of Red Propaganda," *St. Paul Dispatch,* 8 June 1925, 1.

40. Wefald, *A Voice of Protest,* 3, 24, 26. Odd Lovoll has recently added to our knowledge about Norwegian Americans and radicalism in an article detailing the tremendous influence into the 1920s of the Norwegian-language socialist weekly, *Gaa Paa.* See Lovoll, "Gaa Paa: A Scandinavian Voice of Dissent," *Minnesota History* 52 (Fall 1990): 86–100.

41. See Lowell Soike, "Norwegian Americans and the Politics of Dissent, 1890–1924" (Dissertation, University of Iowa, 1980), 24–25.

42. Chrislock, *Ethnicity Challenged,* 116, 120.

43. Chrislock, *The Progressive Era in Minnesota, 1899–1918* (St. Paul: Minnesota Historical Society Press, 1971), 191.

44. Henrik Shipstead to S. H. Holstad, 25 April 1925, Box 2, Norse-American Centennial Papers.

45. Steven J. Keillor, " 'A Remedy Invented by Labor': The Franklin Co-Operative Creamery, 1919–1939," *Minnesota History* 51 (Fall 1989): 259–70.

46. *The Minneapolis Co-Operator* 5 (May 1925): 2.

47. See Keillor, " 'A Remedy Invented by Labor.' "

48. Women's Auxiliary to Executive Committee, 3 January 1925, Box 1, Norse-American Centennial Papers.

49. Mrs. G. H. Niland to Wisconsin Counties, 3 March 1925, Box 3, Norse-American Centennial Papers.

50. Mary Wee to Caroline Storlie, n.d., Box 1, Norse-American Centennial Papers.

51. J. Diesrud to Caroline Storlie, 26 April 1925, Box 2, Norse-American Centennial Papers.

52. Hannah Astrup Larsen, "The First Lady of 'Restaurationen,' " reprinted in Gutterson and Christensen, *Souvenir,* 17, 18.

53. Notes for a speech, 1945, Box 4, Josephine Brack Papers, Norwegian-American Historical Association, Northfield, Minnesota.

54. Minnesota Branch of the National Woman's Party to the Women's Auxiliary, 4 May 1925, Box 2, Norse-American Centennial Papers.

55. See Sara Evans, *Born for Liberty: A History of Women in America* (New York: The Free Press, 1989).

56. Clarence B. Winter to S. H. Holstad, 13 February 1925, Box 1, Norse-American Centennial Papers.

57. George F. Dickson, President of Twin City Manufacturers to Minneapolis Manufacturers, 5 February 1925, Box 1, Norse-American Centennial Papers.

58. Oscar Arneson to Publicity Committee, 21 January 1925, Box 1, Norse-American Centennial Papers.

59. Assistant secretary of the Minneapolis Civic and Commerce Association to S. H. Holstad, 27 April 1925, Box 2, Norse-American Centennial Papers.

60. *Minneapolis Journal*, 5 June 1925, 15, 17.

61. D. H. Bahlrud to Centennial Committee, 11 April 1925, Box 3, Norse-American Centennial Papers.

62. Tollef Quam to Herborg Reque, 21 April 1925, Box 3, Norse-American Centennial Papers.

63. Herborg Reque to Tollef Quam, 25 April 1925, Box 2, Norse-American Centennial Papers.

64. Knut Gjerset to Gisle Bothne, 11 February 1925, Box 1, Norse-American Centennial Papers.

65. Oscar Olson to S. H. Holstad, 12 November 1924, Box 1, Norse-American Centennial Celebration.

66. O. M. Norlie to S. H. Holstad, 23 December, 1924, Box 1, Norse-American Centennial Papers.

67. Anthony Swiatek, "Norse-American Centennial Medal Intriguing," *Coin World*, 30 September 1981, Box 3, Norse-American Centennial Papers.

68. U.S. Congress, House, Medal Commemorative Norse-American Centennial, 1924–25, S. Doc. 1437.

69. Press Release, n.d., Box 3, Norse-American Centennial Papers.

70. Odd Lovoll, " 'The Roaring Twenties': The Emergence of a Norwegian-American Identity," 1990. Unpublished manuscript.

71. Quoted in Pedersen, "Norse-American Centennial," 37.

72. Ibid., 14, 66.

73. Alma A. Gutterson to Centennial Committee, n.d., Box 3, Norse-American Centennial Papers.

74. Gisle Bothne to Lt. Col. Hume, 11 March 1925, Box 1, Norse-American Centennial Papers.

75. Quoted in Pedersen, "Norse-American Centennial," 38.

76. Gustav B. Wollan, "The Saga of Wheatland," Box 4, Norse-American Centennial Papers.

77. Storlie to Local Organizers, 10 December 1924, Norse-American Centennial Daughters Papers, Norwegian-American Historical Association, Northfield, Minnesota.

78. *Minneapolis Journal*, 6 June 1925, 3.

79. Bodnar, *Remaking America*, 17.

80. Oscar L. Olson, copy of speech sent to J. A. Holvik, 9 June 1925, General Correspondence, Johan Andreas Holvik Papers, Minnesota Historical Society, St. Paul, Minnesota.

81. "Pioneers Made Money Ranching, Sons Are Thrifty," *Minneapolis Daily Star*, 8 June 1925, 12.

82. Bulletin #19, 30 May 1925, Box 3, Norse-American Centennial Papers.

83. B. J. Rothnem, *Norwegian-American Centennial Cantata* (Minneapolis: Augsburg Publishing Houses, 1925), 38.

84. Martin W. Odland, "Saga of the Norsemen in America," *Norse-American Centennial*, 31.

85. A Record of the Organization and Incorporation of Norse-American Centennial, Inc., 7 April and 13 May 1925, Box 4, Holvik Papers.

86. Bodnar, *The Transplanted*, 145.

87. Quoted in Pedersen, "Norse-American Centennial," 72.

88. Quoted in ibid., 67.

89. Bulletin #8, 4 April 1925, Box 3, Norse-American Centennial Papers.

90. Press Release, Gustav B. Wollan, n.d., Box 3, Norse-American Centennial Papers.

91. Press Release, n.d., Box 3, Norse-American Centennial Papers.

92. Quoted in Pedersen, "Norse-American Centennial," 106.

93. Quoted in Glassberg, *American Historical Pageantry*, 41.

94. Allesandro Falassi, "Festival: Definition and Morphology," in *Time Out of Time*, 5.

95. See the introduction to Handelman, *Models and Mirrors;* for a discussion of the equal importance of form and performance in public events.

96. Roland Barthes, "Rhetoric of the Images," in *Image/Music/Text,* trans. Stephen Heath (New York: Hill and Wang, 1977), 38.

97. Glassberg, *American Historical Pageantry,* 5, 33, 37, 44.

98. Ibid., 60–61.

99. Ibid., 123.

100. Ibid., 124–26.

101. Ibid., 136, 139, 143.

102. Ibid., 149.

103. Alma Gutterson to Pageant Committee, n.d., Box 3, Norse-American Centennial Papers.

104. Glassberg, *American Historical Pageantry,* 249, 258. Although Glassberg may certainly be correct in his assertion that the public representation of history was no longer "evolutionary" after World War I and certainly not after World War II, his argument that the public use of history serves only a nostalgic function, helping to ease us into modern life, is questionable. As Susan Porter Benson et al. demonstrate so well in *Presenting the Past: Essays on History and the Public* (Philadelphia: Temple University Press, 1986), history is still used for some very concrete, political purposes by people all across the ideological spectrum.

105. Dillman, "Directions for Producing 'Pageant of the Northmen,'" 10.

106. Pedersen, "Norse-American Centennial," 20.

107. George Lipsitz, *Time Passages: Collective Memory and American Popular Culture* (Minneapolis: University of Minnesota Press, 1989), 72.

108. See Victor Turner, "Introduction" and Edith Turner and Victor Turner, "Religious Celebrations," in *Celebrations;* and Moore and Myerhoff, *Symbol and Politics in Communal Ideology.*

5. *"The Nation's Only Safe Foundation"*

1. Gisle Bothne to County Ticket Sellers, Box 3, The Norse-American Centennial Papers.

2. Marianne Mesnil, "Place and Time in Carnivalesque Festival," in Falassi, *Time out of Time*, 190.

3. Falassi, "Festival: Definition and Morphology," in ibid., 2.

4. See Stuart Hall, "Encoding / Decoding," in *Culture, Media, Language*, ed. Stuart Hall et al. (London: Hutchinson, 1980), 128–39.

5. Turner, "Introduction," 16.

6. Roger D. Abrahams, "The Language of Festivals: Celebrating the Economy," in Turner, *Celebrations*, 161.

7. Victor Turner, "Liminality and the Performative Genres," in *Rite, Drama, Festival, Spectacle: Rehearsals Toward a Theory of Cultural Performance*, ed. John MacAloon (Philadelphia: Institute for the Study of Human Issues, 1984), 23.

8. Turner, "Introduction," 18.

9. William A. Wilson, "Herder, Folklore and Romantic Nationalism," in *Folk Groups and Folklore Genres: A Reader*, ed. Elliott Oring (Logan: Utah State University Press, 1989), 22–23.

10. Quoted in Eric Hobsbawm, *Nations and Nationalism since 1780: Programme, Myth, and Reality* (Cambridge: Cambridge University Press, 1990), 12, citing Ernest Renan, *Qu'est ce que c'est une nation?* (Conference faite en Sorbonne le 11 mars 1882) (Paris 1882), 7–8.

11. See Larsen, *A History of Norway* 241–495; and Derry, *A History of Modern Norway, 1814–1972*, 1–171.

12. Wilson, "Herder, Folklore and Romantic Nationalism," 33–35. For an examination of Bjornson's role in Norwegian nationalism, see Harold Larson, *Bjornstjerne Bjornson: A Study in Norwegian Nationalism* (New York: King's Crown Press, 1945).

13. Larsen, *A History of Norway*, 441, 443.

14. Hannah Astrup Larsen, "The First Lady of 'Restaurationen,' " in Gutterson and Christensen, *Souvenir*, 15.

15. Mrs. I. D. Ylvisaker, "Their Gifts," ibid., 47.

16. David W. Noble and David Howard Pitney, "When Prophecy Fails: W. E. B. Du Bois and Charles Beard," Unpublished Manuscript, 2.

17. Rolvaag, "Reflections on Our Heritage," Rolvaag Papers.

18. Ibid.

19. Ibid.

20. Ibid.

21. Ibid.

22. Ibid.

23. George L. Mosse, *The Nationalization of the Masses: Political Symbolism and Mass Movements in Germany from the Napoleonic Wars through the Third Reich* (New York: H. Fertig, 1975), esp. 14–16, 207–16.

24. See Wefald, *A Voice of Protest.*

25. Alma A. Gutterson, "Norway Seen Through the Eyes of an American Tourist," in Gutterson and Christensen, *Souvenir,* 114–20.

26. Rolvaag, "Reflections on Our Heritage," Rolvaag Papers.

27. Axel Johanson to Gisle Bothne, 18 May 1925, Box 1, Gisle Bothne Papers.

28. William Schaunau to Gisle Bothne, 20 April 1925, Box 1, Gisle Bothne Papers.

29. Hobsbawn, *Nations and Nationalism,* 10.

30. Benedict Anderson, *Imagined Communities: Reflections on the Origin and Spread of Nationalism* (London: Verso Editions / NLB, 1983), 15.

31. Hobsbawn, *Nations and Nationalism,* 12.

32. Anderson, *Imagined Communities,* 18–19.

33. Ibid., 31, 131.

34. Ibid., 16.

35. *Minneapolis Sunday Tribune,* 7 June 1925, 1, *Minneapolis Journal,* 5 June 1925, 17, 6 June 1925, 3.

36. Gary Gerstle, *Working-Class Americanism: The Politics of Labor in a Textile City, 1914–1960* (New York: Cambridge University Press, 1989), 6–8.

37. See Mary Ryan, "Gender and Public Access: Women's Politics in Nineteenth-Century America," in Calhoun, *Habermas and the Public Sphere,* 259–89; and Ryan, *Women in the Public: Between Banners and Ballots, 1825–1880* (Baltimore: Johns Hopkins University Press, 1990). For a fuller discussion of the scholarship on "counterpublics," see Fraser, "Rethinking the Public Sphere," 109–42.

38. Anderson, *Imagined Communities,* 132.

39. Mrs. John O. Lee, "The 'Living Flag,' " 122.

40. Anderson, *Imagined Communities,* 140.

41. Leif Gilstad, "Tiny Norse Mayflower's Voyage 100 Years Ago Brings World's Biggest 1925 Gathering to City," *Minneapolis Journal,* 31 May 1925, Editorial Section, 1.

42. *Minneapolis Tribune,* 7 June 1925, 1.

43. *Minneapolis Journal,* 3 June 1925, 11.

44. Mrs. A. Minger to Committee, 25 January 1925, Box 1, Norse-American Centennial Papers.

45. F. Engbretsen to Bothne, 26 August 1924, Box 1, Gisle Bothne Papers.

46. Quoted from *Nordisk Tidende* in "The Norse-American Centennial," 24. Other quotations also from "The Norse-American Centennial," 72, 30.

47. Turner, "Liminality and the Performative Genres," 20.

48. Bertha Law Dahls to Caroline Storlie, Box 1, Norse-American Centennial Daughters Papers.

49. Letter to Committee, September 1924, Box 1, Norse-American Centennial Papers.

50. Annalia Winger to Bothne, 6 June 1925, Box 1, Norse-American Centennial Papers.

51. Ragna Grimsby to Committee, Box 3, Norse-American Centennial Papers.

52. Exhibition Catalogue, Box 7, Norse-American Centennial Papers.

53. Camella Hardy to Mabel Leland, 4 April 1925, Box 2, Norse-American Centennial Papers.

54. Mrs. J. E. Norswing to Herborg Reque, 3 May 1925, Box 2, Norse-American Centennial Papers.

55. Anna B. Parker to Storlie, Box 3, Norse-American Centennial Papers.

56. Mrs. William McCulloch to Women's Committee, 4 April 1925, Box 2, Norse-American Centennial Papers.

57. Mrs. Moe to Committee, 14 January 1925, Box 1, Norse-American Centennial Papers.

58. Quoted in Pedersen, "The Norse-American Centennial," 106.

59. *Norse-American Centennial, 1825–1925: Souvenir Edition* (Minneapolis, 1925).

60. O. M. Norlie, "Why We Celebrate," 51–52.

61. Ibid., 56.

62. George Sverdrup to Gisle Bothne, 7 November 1924; O. M. Norlie to Gisle Bothne, 10 December 1924, Box 1, Norse-American Centennial Papers; *Norse-American Centennial*, 54–55.

63. Falassi, "Festival: Definition and Morphology," 5.

64. Waldemar Ager, "Reflections on Our Centennial," trans. Kristian Bogen in the author's possession, *Norse-American Centennial*, 12–13.

65. Rolvaag, "Reflection on Our Heritage."

66. Rolvaag, *Their Father's God* (Lincoln: University of Nebraska Press, 1982), 206, 210.

67. Paul Reigstad, "Rolvaag as Myth-Maker," *Ole Rolvaag: Artist and Cultural Leader* (Northfield: St. Olaf College Press, 1975), 59.

68. Turner, "Introduction," 21.

69. Michael Bristol, "Carnival and the Institution of Theatre in Elizabethan England," *English Literary History* 50 (1983): 638; see also Michael Bristol, *Carnival and Theater: Plebeian Culture and the Structure of Authority in Renaissance England* (New York: Methuen, 1985).

70. Sally Falk Moore, "Epilogue," in Moore and Myerhoff, *Symbol and Politics in Communal Ideology*, 234.

71. Bristol, "Carnival and the Institution of Theatre", 640.

72. Gary Saul Morson, "Who Speaks for Bakhtin?: A Dialogic Introduction," *Critical Inquiry* 10 (Oct/Dec 1983): 228. For Bakhtin's concept of carnival and the dialogic, see especially Mikhail Bakhtin, *Rabelais and His World*, trans. Helene Iswolsky (Bloomington: Indiana University Press, 1984); and Bakhtin, *The Dialogic Imagination*, trans. Michael Holquist and Caryl Emerson (Austin: University of Texas Press, 1981).

73. Dillmann, "Directions for Producing 'Pageant of the Northmen,' " 11–12.

74. Fischer, "Ethnicity and the Post-Modern Arts of Memory," 20.

75. Glassberg, *American Historical Pageantry*, 246.

76. Ibid., 132–33.

Conclusion

1. Walter Benjamin, "Theses on the Philosophy of History," in *Illuminations*, ed. Hannah Arendt (New York: Harcourt and Brace, 1978), 257.

2. See, for example, Hall, "The Narrative Construction of Reality," 3–17.

3. Michael Frisch, "The Memory of History," in *Presenting the Past: Essays on History and the Public*, ed. Susan Porter Benson, Stephen Brier, Roy Rosenzweig (Philadelphia: Temple University Press, 1986), 6. See also Bodnar, *Remaking America*.

4. Lipsitz, *Time Passages*, 34.

5. Jan Assmann, "Guilt and Remembrance: On the Theologization of History in the Ancient Near East," *History and Memory: Studies in Representation of the Past* 2 (Fall 1990): 7.

6. Lipsitz, *Time Passages*, 34.

7. See particularly W. Lloyd Warner, *Yankee City Series* (New Haven: Yale University Press, 1959), vol. 5, *The Living and the Dead: A Study of the Symbolic Life of Americans*.

8. Assmann, "Guilt and Remembrance," 9–10.

9. See, for example, Virginia Yans-McLaughlin, *Family and Community: Italian Immigrants in Buffalo, 1880–1930* (Ithaca: Cornell University Press, 1977).

10. Bodnar, *Remaking America*, 71.

11. See Anderson, *Imagined Communities*; Hobsbawm, *Nations and Nationalism*; and Mosse, *The Nationalization of the Masses*.

12. Hobsbawm, *The Invention of Tradition*.

13. D. G. Ristad, "The Norwegian-American Historical Association," *Norwegian-American Historical Association Studies and Records* 1 (1926): 148.

14. See especially O. M. Norlie, *A History of the Norwegian People in America* (1925); Theodore Blegen, *Norwegian Migration to America: The American Transition* (1940); and Carl Chrislock, *Ethnicity Challenged: The Upper Midwest Norwegian-American Experience in WWI* (1981).

15. Herbert Gans, "Symbolic Ethnicity: The Future of Ethnic Groups and Cultures in America," *Ethnic and Racial Studies* 2 (January 1979): 1–20.

16. Mary C. Waters, *Ethnic Options: Choosing Identities in America* (Berkeley: University of California Press, 1990). See also Richard D. Alba, *Ethnic Identity: The Transformation of White America* (New Haven: Yale University Press, 1990). Alba argues that such "symbolic ethnicity" among whites is part of an emergent "European American" ethnicity. Waters found that the meanings attached to being Irish, Italian, German, or a combination of ethnic heritages, were very similar in their emphases on family and community. Alba points out that these similarities point to a "European American" ethnicity that has created its own mythology about its history, a history that, as Waters argues, has important ideological ramifications for minority ethnic groups.

Index

✤